The Poetry of Algernon Charles Swinburne

VOLUME VI – POEMS AND BALLADS (SECOND SERIES)

Algernon Charles Swinburne was born on April 5th, 1837, in London, into a wealthy Northumbrian family. He was educated at Eton and at Balliol College, Oxford, but did not complete a degree.

In 1860 Swinburne published two verse dramas but achieved his first literary success in 1865 with Atalanta in Calydon, written in the form of classical Greek tragedy. The following year "Poems and Ballads" brought him instant notoriety. He was now identified with "indecent" themes and the precept of art for art's sake.

Although he produced much after this success in general his popularity and critical reputation declined. The most important qualities of Swinburne's work are an intense lyricism, his intricately extended and evocative imagery, metrical virtuosity, rich use of assonance and alliteration, and bold, complex rhythms.

Swinburne's physical appearance was small, frail, and plagued by several other oddities of physique and temperament. Throughout the 1860s and 1870s he drank excessively and was prone to accidents that often left him bruised, bloody, or unconscious. Until his forties he suffered intermittent physical collapses that necessitated removal to his parents' home while he recovered.

Throughout his career Swinburne also published literary criticism of great worth. His deep knowledge of world literatures contributed to a critical style rich in quotation, allusion, and comparison. He is particularly noted for discerning studies of Elizabethan dramatists and of many English and French poets and novelists. As well he was a noted essayist and wrote two novels.

In 1879, Swinburne's friend and literary agent, Theodore Watts-Dunton, intervened during a time when Swinburne was dangerously ill. Watts-Dunton isolated Swinburne at a suburban home in Putney and gradually weaned him from alcohol, former companions and many other habits as well.

Much of his poetry in this period may be inferior but some individual poems are exceptional; "By the North Sea," "Evening on the Broads," "A Nympholept," "The Lake of Gaube," and "Neap-Tide."

Swinburne lived another thirty years with Watts-Dunton. He denied Swinburne's friends access to him, controlled the poet's money, and restricted his activities. It is often quoted that 'he saved the man but killed the poet'.

Swinburne died on April 10th, 1909 at the age of seventy-two.

Index of Contents

INSCRIBED TO RICHARD F. BURTON

IN REDEMPTION OF AN OLD PLEDGE AND IN RECOGNITION OF A FRIENDSHIP WHICH I MUST ALWAYS COUNT AMONG THE HIGHEST HONOURS OF MY LIFE

THE LAST ORACLE

(A.D. 361)

[Greek:
eipate tô basilêi, chamai pese daidalos aula;
ouketi Phoibos echei kaluban, ou mantida daphnên,
ou pagan laleousan; apesbeto kai lalon hudôr.]

Years have risen and fallen in darkness or in twilight,
Ages waxed and waned that knew not thee nor thine,
While the world sought light by night and sought not thy light,
Since the sad last pilgrim left thy dark mid shrine.
Dark the shrine and dumb the fount of song thence welling,
Save for words more sad than tears of blood, that said:
Tell the king, on earth has fallen the glorious dwelling,
And the watersprings that spake are quenched and dead.
Not a cell is left the God, no roof, no cover
In his hand the prophet laurel flowers no more.
And the great king's high sad heart, thy true last lover,
Felt thine answer pierce and cleave it to the core.
And he bowed down his hopeless head
In the drift of the wild world's tide,
And dying, Thou hast conquered, he said,
Galilean; he said it, and died.
And the world that was thine and was ours

When the Graces took hands with the Hours
Grew cold as a winter wave
In the wind from a wide-mouthed grave,
As a gulf wide open to swallow
The light that the world held dear.
O father of all of us, Paian, Apollo,
Destroyer and healer, hear!

Age on age thy mouth was mute, thy face was hidden,
And the lips and eyes that loved thee blind and dumb;
Song forsook their tongues that held thy name forbidden,
Light their eyes that saw the strange God's kingdom come.
Fire for light and hell for heaven and psalms for pæans
Filled the clearest eyes and lips most sweet of song,
When for chant of Greeks the wail of Galileans
Made the whole world moan with hymns of wrath and wrong.
Yea, not yet we see thee, father, as they saw thee,
They that worshipped when the world was theirs and thine,
They whose words had power by thine own power to draw thee
Down from heaven till earth seemed more than heaven divine.
For the shades are about us that hover
When darkness is half withdrawn
And the skirts of the dead night cover
The face of the live new dawn.
For the past is not utterly past
Though the word on its lips be the last,
And the time be gone by with its creed
When men were as beasts that bleed,
As sheep or as swine that wallow,
In the shambles of faith and of fear.
O father of all of us, Paian, Apollo,
Destroyer and healer, hear!

Yet it may be, lord and father, could we know it,
We that love thee for our darkness shall have light
More than ever prophet hailed of old or poet
Standing crowned and robed and sovereign in thy sight.
To the likeness of one God their dreams enthralled thee,
Who wast greater than all Gods that waned and grew;
Son of God the shining son of Time they called thee,
Who wast older, O our father, than they knew.
For no thought of man made Gods to love or honour
Ere the song within the silent soul began,
Nor might earth in dream or deed take heaven upon her
Till the word was clothed with speech by lips of man.
And the word and the life wast thou,
The spirit of man and the breath;
And before thee the Gods that bow

Take life at thine hands and death.
For these are as ghosts that wane,
That are gone in an age or twain;
Harsh, merciful, passionate, pure,
They perish, but thou shalt endure;
Be their flight with the swan or the swallow,
They pass as the flight of a year.
O father of all of us, Paian, Apollo,
Destroyer and healer, hear!

Thou the word, the light, the life, the breath, the glory,
Strong to help and heal, to lighten and to slay,
Thine is all the song of man, the world's whole story;
Not of morning and of evening is thy day.
Old and younger Gods are buried or begotten
From uprising to downsetting of thy sun,
Risen from eastward, fallen to westward and forgotten,
And their springs are many, but their end is one.
Divers births of godheads find one death appointed,
As the soul whence each was born makes room for each;
God by God goes out, discrowned and disanointed,
But the soul stands fast that gave them shape and speech.
Is the sun yet cast out of heaven?
Is the song yet cast out of man?
Life that had song for its leaven
To quicken the blood that ran
Through the veins of the songless years
More bitter and cold than tears,
Heaven that had thee for its one
Light, life, word, witness, O sun,
Are they soundless and sightless and hollow,
Without eye, without speech, without ear?
O father of all of us, Paian, Apollo,
Destroyer and healer, hear!

Time arose and smote thee silent at his warning,
Change and darkness fell on men that fell from thee;
Dark thou satest, veiled with light, behind the morning,
Till the soul of man should lift up eyes and see.
Till the blind mute soul get speech again and eyesight,
Man may worship not the light of life within;
In his sight the stars whose fires grow dark in thy sight
Shine as sunbeams on the night of death and sin.
Time again is risen with mightier word of warning,
Change hath blown again a blast of louder breath;
Clothed with clouds and stars and dreams that melt in morning,
Lo, the Gods that ruled by grace of sin and death!
They are conquered, they break, they are stricken,

Whose might made the whole world pale;
They are dust that shall rise not or quicken
Though the world for their death's sake wail.
As a hound on a wild beast's trace,
So time has their godhead in chase;
As wolves when the hunt makes head,
They are scattered, they fly, they are fled;
They are fled beyond hail, beyond hollo,
And the cry of the chase, and the cheer.
O father of all of us, Paian, Apollo,
Destroyer and healer, hear!

Day by day thy shadow shines in heaven beholden,
Even the sun, the shining shadow of thy face:
King, the ways of heaven before thy feet grow golden;
God, the soul of earth is kindled with thy grace.
In thy lips the speech of man whence Gods were fashioned,
In thy soul the thought that makes them and unmakes;
By thy light and heat incarnate and impassioned,
Soul to soul of man gives light for light and takes.
As they knew thy name of old time could we know it,
Healer called of sickness, slayer invoked of wrong,
Light of eyes that saw thy light, God, king, priest, poet,
Song should bring thee back to heal us with thy song.
For thy kingdom is past not away,
Nor thy power from the place thereof hurled;
Out of heaven they shall cast not the day,
They shall cast not out song from the world.
By the song and the light they give
We know thy works that they live;
With the gift thou hast given us of speech
We praise, we adore, we beseech,
We arise at thy bidding and follow,
We cry to thee, answer, appear,
O father of all of us, Paian, Apollo,
Destroyer and healer, hear!

IN THE BAY

I

Beyond the hollow sunset, ere a star
Take heart in heaven from eastward, while the west,
Fulfilled of watery resonance and rest,
Is as a port with clouds for harbour bar
To fold the fleet in of the winds from far

That stir no plume now of the bland sea's breast:

II

Above the soft sweep of the breathless bay
Southwestward, far past flight of night and day,
Lower than the sunken sunset sinks, and higher
Than dawn can freak the front of heaven with fire,
My thought with eyes and wings made wide makes way
To find the place of souls that I desire.

III

If any place for any soul there be,
Disrobed and disentrammelled; if the might,
The fire and force that filled with ardent light
The souls whose shadow is half the light we see,
Survive and be suppressed not of the night;
This hour should show what all day hid from me.

IV

Night knows not, neither is it shown to day,
By sunlight nor by starlight is it shown,
Nor to the full moon's eye nor footfall known,
Their world's untrodden and unkindled way.
Nor is the breath nor music of it blown
With sounds of winter or with winds of May.

V

But here, where light and darkness reconciled
Hold earth between them as a weanling child
Between the balanced hands of death and birth,
Even as they held the new-born shape of earth
When first life trembled in her limbs and smiled,
Here hope might think to find what hope were worth.

VI

Past Hades, past Elysium, past the long
Slow smooth strong lapse of Lethe—past the toil
Wherein all souls are taken as a spoil,

The Stygian web of waters—if your song
Be quenched not, O our brethren, but be strong
As ere ye too shook off our temporal coil;

VII

If yet these twain survive your worldly breath,
Joy trampling sorrow, life devouring death,
If perfect life possess your life all through
And like your words your souls be deathless too,
To-night, of all whom night encompasseth,
My soul would commune with one soul of you.

VIII

Above the sunset might I see thine eyes
That were above the sundawn in our skies,
Son of the songs of morning,—thine that were
First lights to lighten that rekindling air
Wherethrough men saw the front of England rise
And heard thine loudest of the lyre-notes there—

IX

If yet thy fire have not one spark the less,
O Titan, born of her a Titaness,
Across the sunrise and the sunset's mark
Send of thy lyre one sound, thy fire one spark,
To change this face of our unworthiness,
Across this hour dividing light from dark.

X

To change this face of our chill time, that hears
No song like thine of all that crowd its ears,
Of all its lights that lighten all day long
Sees none like thy most fleet and fiery sphere's
Outlightening Sirius—in its twilight throng
No thunder and no sunrise like thy song.

XI

Hath not the sea-wind swept the sea-line bare

To pave with stainless fire through stainless air
A passage for thine heavenlier feet to tread
Ungrieved of earthly floor-work? hath it spread
No covering splendid as the sun-god's hair
To veil or to reveal thy lordlier head?

XII

Hath not the sunset strewn across the sea
A way majestical enough for thee?
What hour save this should be thine hour—and mine,
If thou have care of any less divine
Than thine own soul; if thou take thought of me,
Marlowe, as all my soul takes thought of thine?

XIII

Before the moon's face as before the sun
The morning star and evening star are one
For all men's lands as England. O, if night
Hang hard upon us,—ere our day take flight,
Shed thou some comfort from thy day long done
On us pale children of the latter light!

XIV

For surely, brother and master and lord and king,
Where'er thy footfall and thy face make spring
In all souls' eyes that meet thee wheresoe'er,
And have thy soul for sunshine and sweet air—
Some late love of thine old live land should cling,
Some living love of England, round thee there.

XV

Here from her shore across her sunniest sea
My soul makes question of the sun for thee,
And waves and beams make answer. When thy feet
Made her ways flowerier and their flowers more sweet
With childlike passage of a god to be,
Like spray these waves cast off her foemen's fleet.

XVI

Like foam they flung it from her, and like weed
Its wrecks were washed from scornful shoal to shoal,
From rock to rock reverberate; and the whole
Sea laughed and lightened with a deathless deed
That sowed our enemies in her field for seed
And made her shores fit harbourage for thy soul.

XVII

Then in her green south fields, a poor man's child,
Thou hadst thy short sweet fill of half-blown joy,
That ripens all of us for time to cloy
With full-blown pain and passion; ere the wild
World caught thee by the fiery heart, and smiled
To make so swift end of the godlike boy.

XVIII

For thou, if ever godlike foot there trod
These fields of ours, wert surely like a god.
Who knows what splendour of strange dreams was shed
With sacred shadow and glimmer of gold and red
From hallowed windows, over stone and sod,
On thine unbowed bright insubmissive head?

XIX

The shadow stayed not, but the splendour stays,
Our brother, till the last of English days.
No day nor night on English earth shall be
For ever, spring nor summer, Junes nor Mays,
But somewhat as a sound or gleam of thee
Shall come on us like morning from the sea.

XX

Like sunrise never wholly risen, nor yet
Quenched; or like sunset never wholly set,
A light to lighten as from living eyes
The cold unlit close lids of one that lies
Dead, or a ray returned from death's far skies
To fire us living lest our lives forget.

XXI

For in that heaven what light of lights may be,
What splendour of what stars, what spheres of flame
Sounding, that none may number nor may name,
We know not, even thy brethren; yea, not we
Whose eyes desire the light that lightened thee,
Whose ways and thine are one way and the same.

XXII

But if the riddles that in sleep we read,
And trust them not, be flattering truth indeed,
As he that rose our mightiest called them,—he,
Much higher than thou as thou much higher than we—
There, might we say, all flower of all our seed,
All singing souls are as one sounding sea.

XXIII

All those that here were of thy kind and kin,
Beside thee and below thee, full of love,
Full-souled for song,—and one alone above
Whose only light folds all your glories in—
With all birds' notes from nightingale to dove
Fill the world whither we too fain would win.

XXIV

The world that sees in heaven the sovereign light
Of sunlike Shakespeare, and the fiery night
Whose stars were watched of Webster; and beneath,
The twin-souled brethren of the single wreath,
Grown in kings' gardens, plucked from pastoral heath,
Wrought with all flowers for all men's heart's delight.

XXV

And that fixed fervour, iron-red like Mars,
In the mid moving tide of tenderer stars,
That burned on loves and deeds the darkest done,
Athwart the incestuous prisoner's bride-house bars;
And thine, most highest of all their fires but one,

Our morning star, sole risen before the sun.

XXVI

And one light risen since theirs to run such race
Thou hast seen, O Phosphor, from thy pride of place.
Thou hast seen Shelley, him that was to thee
As light to fire or dawn to lightning; me,
Me likewise, O our brother, shalt thou see,
And I behold thee, face to glorious face?

XXVII

You twain the same swift year of manhood swept
Down the steep darkness, and our father wept.
And from the gleam of Apollonian tears
A holier aureole rounds your memories, kept
Most fervent-fresh of all the singing spheres,
And April-coloured through all months and years.

XXVIII

You twain fate spared not half your fiery span;
The longer date fulfils the lesser man.
Ye from beyond the dark dividing date
Stand smiling, crowned as gods with foot on fate.
For stronger was your blessing than his ban,
And earliest whom he struck, he struck too late.

XXIX

Yet love and loathing, faith and unfaith yet
Bind less to greater souls in unison,
And one desire that makes three spirits as one
Takes great and small as in one spiritual net
Woven out of hope toward what shall yet be done
Ere hate or love remember or forget.

XXX

Woven out of faith and hope and love too great
To bear the bonds of life and death and fate:
Woven out of love and hope and faith too dear

To take the print of doubt and change and fear:
And interwoven with lines of wrath and hate
Blood-red with soils of many a sanguine year.

XXXI

Who cannot hate, can love not; if he grieve,
His tears are barren as the unfruitful rain
That rears no harvest from the green sea's plain,
And as thorns crackling this man's laugh is vain.
Nor can belief touch, kindle, smite, reprieve
His heart who has not heart to disbelieve.

XXXII

But you, most perfect in your hate and love,
Our great twin-spirited brethren; you that stand
Head by head glittering, hand made fast in hand,
And underfoot the fang-drawn worm that strove
To wound you living; from so far above,
Look love, not scorn, on ours that was your land.

XXXIII

For love we lack, and help and heat and light
To clothe us and to comfort us with might.
What help is ours to take or give? but ye—
O, more than sunrise to the blind cold sea,
That wailed aloud with all her waves all night,
Much more, being much more glorious, should you be.

XXXIV

As fire to frost, as ease to toil, as dew
To flowerless fields, as sleep to slackening pain,
As hope to souls long weaned from hope again
Returning, or as blood revived anew
To dry-drawn limbs and every pulseless vein,
Even so toward us should no man be but you.

XXXV

One rose before the sunrise was, and one

Before the sunset, lovelier than the sun.
And now the heaven is dark and bright and loud
With wind and starry drift and moon and cloud,
And night's cry rings in straining sheet and shroud,
What help is ours if hope like yours be none?

XXXVI

O well-beloved, our brethren, if ye be,
Then are we not forsaken. This kind earth
Made fragrant once for all time with your birth,
And bright for all men with your love, and worth
The clasp and kiss and wedlock of the sea,
Were not your mother if not your brethren we.

XXXVII

Because the days were dark with gods and kings
And in time's hand the old hours of time as rods,
When force and fear set hope and faith at odds,
Ye failed not nor abased your plume-plucked wings;
And we that front not more disastrous things,
How should we fail in face of kings and gods?

XXXVIII

For now the deep dense plumes of night are thinned
Surely with winnowing of the glimmering wind
Whose feet are fledged with morning; and the breath
Begins in heaven that sings the dark to death.
And all the night wherein men groaned and sinned
Sickens at heart to hear what sundawn saith.

XXXIX

O first-born sons of hope and fairest, ye
Whose prows first clove the thought-unsounded sea
Whence all the dark dead centuries rose to bar
The spirit of man lest truth should make him free,
The sunrise and the sunset, seeing one star,
Take heart as we to know you that ye are.

XL

Ye rise not and ye set not; we that say
Ye rise and set like hopes that set and rise
Look yet but seaward from a land-locked bay;
But where at last the sea's line is the sky's
And truth and hope one sunlight in your eyes,
No sunrise and no sunset marks their day.

A FORSAKEN GARDEN

In a coign of the cliff between lowland and highland,
At the sea-down's edge between windward and lee,
Walled round with rocks as an inland island,
The ghost of a garden fronts the sea.
A girdle of brushwood and thorn encloses
The steep square slope of the blossomless bed
Where the weeds that grew green from the graves of its roses
Now lie dead.

The fields fall southward, abrupt and broken,
To the low last edge of the long lone land.
If a step should sound or a word be spoken,
Would a ghost not rise at the strange guest's hand?
So long have the grey bare walks lain guestless,
Through branches and briars if a man make way,
He shall find no life but the sea-wind's, restless
Night and day.

The dense hard passage is blind and stifled
That crawls by a track none turn to climb
To the strait waste place that the years have rifled
Of all but the thorns that are touched not of time.
The thorns he spares when the rose is taken;
The rocks are left when he wastes the plain.
The wind that wanders, the weeds wind-shaken,
These remain.

Not a flower to be pressed of the foot that falls not;
As the heart of a dead man the seed-plots are dry;
From the thicket of thorns whence the nightingale calls not,
Could she call, there were never a rose to reply.
Over the meadows that blossom and wither
Rings but the note of a sea-bird's song;
Only the sun and the rain come hither
All year long.

The sun burns sere and the rain dishevels
One gaunt bleak blossom of scentless breath.
Only the wind here hovers and revels
In a round where life seems barren as death.
Here there was laughing of old, there was weeping,
Haply, of lovers none ever will know,
Whose eyes went seaward a hundred sleeping
Years ago.

Heart handfast in heart as they stood, "Look thither,"
Did he whisper? "look forth from the flowers to the sea;
For the foam-flowers endure when the rose-blossoms wither,
And men that love lightly may die—but we?"
And the same wind sang and the same waves whitened,
And or ever the garden's last petals were shed,
In the lips that had whispered, the eyes that had lightened,
Love was dead.

Or they loved their life through, and then went whither?
And were one to the end—but what end who knows?
Love deep as the sea as a rose must wither,
As the rose-red seaweed that mocks the rose.
Shall the dead take thought for the dead to love them?
What love was ever as deep as a grave?
They are loveless now as the grass above them
Or the wave.

All are at one now, roses and lovers,
Not known of the cliffs and the fields and the sea.
Not a breath of the time that has been hovers
In the air now soft with a summer to be.
Not a breath shall there sweeten the seasons hereafter
Of the flowers or the lovers that laugh now or weep,
When as they that are free now of weeping and laughter
We shall sleep.

Here death may deal not again for ever;
Here change may come not till all change end.
From the graves they have made they shall rise up never,
Who have left nought living to ravage and rend.
Earth, stones, and thorns of the wild ground growing,
While the sun and the rain live, these shall be;
Till a last wind's breath upon all these blowing
Roll the sea.

Till the slow sea rise and the sheer cliff crumble,
Till terrace and meadow the deep gulfs drink,
Till the strength of the waves of the high tides humble

The fields that lessen, the rocks that shrink,
Here now in his triumph where all things falter,
Stretched out on the spoils that his own hand spread,
As a god self-slain on his own strange altar,
Death lies dead.

RELICS

This flower that smells of honey and the sea,
White laurustine, seems in my hand to be
A white star made of memory long ago
Lit in the heaven of dear times dead to me.

A star out of the skies love used to know
Here held in hand, a stray left yet to show
What flowers my heart was full of in the days
That are long since gone down dead memory's flow.

Dead memory that revives on doubtful ways,
Half hearkening what the buried season says
Out of the world of the unapparent dead
Where the lost Aprils are, and the lost Mays.

Flower, once I knew thy star-white brethren bred
Nigh where the last of all the land made head
Against the sea, a keen-faced promontory,
Flowers on salt wind and sprinkled sea-dews fed.

Their hearts were glad of the free place's glory;
The wind that sang them all his stormy story
Had talked all winter to the sleepless spray,
And as the sea's their hues were hard and hoary.

Like things born of the sea and the bright day,
They laughed out at the years that could not slay,
Live sons and joyous of unquiet hours,
And stronger than all storms that range for prey.

And in the close indomitable flowers
A keen-edged odour of the sun and showers
Was as the smell of the fresh honeycomb
Made sweet for mouths of none but paramours.

Out of the hard green wall of leaves that clomb
They showed like windfalls of the snow-soft foam,
Or feathers from the weary south-wind's wing,

Fair as the spray that it came shoreward from.

And thou, as white, what word hast thou to bring?
If my heart hearken, whereof wilt thou sing?
For some sign surely thou too hast to bear,
Some word far south was taught thee of the spring.

White like a white rose, not like these that were
Taught of the wind's mouth and the winter air,
Poor tender thing of soft Italian bloom,
Where once thou grewest, what else for me grew there?

Born in what spring and on what city's tomb,
By whose hand wast thou reached, and plucked for whom?
There hangs about thee, could the soul's sense tell,
An odour as of love and of love's doom.

Of days more sweet than thou wast sweet to smell,
Of flower-soft thoughts that came to flower and fell,
Of loves that lived a lily's life and died,
Of dreams now dwelling where dead roses dwell.

O white birth of the golden mountain-side
That for the sun's love makes its bosom wide
At sunrise, and with all its woods and flowers
Takes in the morning to its heart of pride!

Thou hast a word of that one land of ours,
And of the fair town called of the Fair Towers,
A word for me of my San Gimignan,
A word of April's greenest-girdled hours.

Of the old breached walls whereon the wallflowers ran
Called of Saint Fina, breachless now of man,
Though time with soft feet break them stone by stone,
Who breaks down hour by hour his own reign's span.

Of the old cliff overcome and overgrown
That all that flowerage clothed as flesh clothes bone,
That garment of acacias made for May,
Whereof here lies one witness overblown.

The fair brave trees with all their flowers at play,
How king-like they stood up into the day!
How sweet the day was with them, and the night!
Such words of message have dead flowers to say.

This that the winter and the wind made bright,

And this that lived upon Italian light,
Before I throw them and these words away,
Who knows but I what memories too take flight?

AT A MONTH'S END

The night last night was strange and shaken:
More strange the change of you and me.
Once more, for the old love's love forsaken,
We went out once more toward the sea.

For the old love's love-sake dead and buried,
One last time, one more and no more,
We watched the waves set in, the serried
Spears of the tide storming the shore.

Hardly we saw the high moon hanging,
Heard hardly through the windy night
Far waters ringing, low reefs clanging,
Under wan skies and waste white light.

With chafe and change of surges chiming,
The clashing channels rocked and rang
Large music, wave to wild wave timing,
And all the choral water sang.

Faint lights fell this way, that way floated,
Quick sparks of sea-fire keen like eyes
From the rolled surf that flashed, and noted
Shores and faint cliffs and bays and skies.

The ghost of sea that shrank up sighing
At the sand's edge, a short sad breath
Trembling to touch the goal, and dying
With weak heart heaved up once in death—

The rustling sand and shingle shaken
With light sweet touches and small sound—
These could not move us, could not waken
Hearts to look forth, eyes to look round.

Silent we went an hour together,
Under grey skies by waters white.
Our hearts were full of windy weather,
Clouds and blown stars and broken light.

Full of cold clouds and moonbeams drifted
And streaming storms and straying fires,
Our souls in us were stirred and shifted
By doubts and dreams and foiled desires.

Across, aslant, a scudding sea-mew
Swam, dipped, and dropped, and grazed the sea:
And one with me I could not dream you;
And one with you I could not be.

As the white wing the white wave's fringes
Touched and slid over and flashed past—
As a pale cloud a pale flame tinges
From the moon's lowest light and last—

As a star feels the sun and falters,
Touched to death by diviner eyes—
As on the old gods' untended altars
The old lire of withered worship dies—

(Once only, once the shrine relighted
Sees the last fiery shadow shine,
Last shadow of flame and faith benighted,
Sees falter and flutter and fail the shrine)

So once with fiery breath and flying
Your winged heart touched mine and went,
And the swift spirits kissed, and sighing,
Sundered and smiled and were content.

That only touch, that feeling only,
Enough we found, we found too much;
For the unlit shrine is hardly lonely
As one the old fire forgets to touch.

Slight as the sea's sight of the sea-mew,
Slight as the sun's sight of the star:
Enough to show one must not deem you
For love's sake other than you are.

Who snares and tames with fear and danger
A bright beast of a fiery kin,
Only to mar, only to change her
Sleek supple soul and splendid skin?

Easy with blows to mar and maim her,
Easy with bonds to bind and bruise;
What profit, if she yield her tamer

The limbs to mar, the soul to lose?

Best leave or take the perfect creature,
Take all she is or leave complete;
Transmute you will not form or feature,
Change feet for wings or wings for feet.

Strange eyes, new limbs, can no man give her;
Sweet is the sweet thing as it is.
No soul she hath, we see, to outlive her;
Hath she for that no lips to kiss?

So may one read his weird, and reason,
And with vain drugs assuage no pain.
For each man in his loving season
Fools and is fooled of these in vain.

Charms that allay not any longing,
Spells that appease not any grief,
Time brings us all by handfuls, wronging
All hurts with nothing of relief.

Ah, too soon shot, the fool's bolt misses!
What help? the world is full of loves;
Night after night of running kisses,
Chirp after chirp of changing doves.

Should Love disown or disesteem you
For loving one man more or less?
You could not tame your light white sea-mew,
Nor I my sleek black pantheress.

For a new soul let whoso please pray,
We are what life made us, and shall be.
For you the jungle and me the sea-spray,
And south for you and north for me.

But this one broken foam-white feather
I throw you off the hither wing,
Splashed stiff with sea-scurf and salt weather,
This song for sleep to learn and sing—

Sing in your ear when, daytime over,
You, couched at long length on hot sand
With some sleek sun-discoloured lover,
Wince from his breach as from a brand:

Till the acrid hour aches out and ceases,

And the sheathed eyeball sleepier swims,
The deep flank smoothes its dimpling creases.
And passion loosens all the limbs:

Till dreams of sharp grey north-sea weather
Fall faint upon your fiery sleep,
As on strange sands a strayed bird's feather
The wind may choose to lose or keep.

But I, who leave my queen of panthers,
As a tired honey-heavy bee
Gilt with sweet dust from gold-grained anthers
Leaves the rose-chalice, what for me?

From the ardours of the chaliced centre,
From the amorous anthers' golden grime,
That scorch and smutch all wings that enter,
I fly forth hot from honey-time.

But as to a bee's gilt thighs and winglets
The flower-dust with the flower-smell clings;
As a snake's mobile rampant ringlets
Leave the sand marked with print of rings;

So to my soul in surer fashion
Your savage stamp and savour hangs;
The print and perfume of old passion,
The wild-beast mark of panther's fangs.

SESTINA

I saw my soul at rest upon a day
As a bird sleeping in the nest of night,
Among soft leaves that give the starlight way
To touch its wings but not its eyes with light;
So that it knew as one in visions may,
And knew not as men waking, of delight.

This was the measure of my soul's delight;
It had no power of joy to fly by day,
Nor part in the large lordship of the light;
But in a secret moon-beholden way
Had all its will of dreams and pleasant night,
And all the love and life that sleepers may.

But such life's triumph as men waking may

It might not have to feed its faint delight
Between the stars by night and sun by day,
Shut up with green leaves and a little light;
Because its way was as a lost star's way,
A world's not wholly known of day or night.

All loves and dreams and sounds and gleams of night
Made it all music that such minstrels may,
And all they had they gave it of delight;
But in the full face of the fire of day
What place shall be for any starry light,
What part of heaven in all the wide sun's way?

Yet the soul woke not, sleeping by the way,
Watched as a nursling of the large-eyed night,
And sought no strength nor knowledge of the day,
Nor closer touch conclusive of delight,
Nor mightier joy nor truer than dreamers may,
Nor more of song than they, nor more of light.

For who sleeps once and sees the secret light
Whereby sleep shows the soul a fairer way
Between the rise and rest of day and night,
Shall care no more to fare as all men may,
But be his place of pain or of delight,
There shall he dwell, beholding night as day.

Song, have thy day and take thy fill of light
Before the night be fallen across thy way;
Sing while he may, man hath no long delight.

THE YEAR OF THE ROSE

From the depths of the green garden-closes
Where the summer in darkness dozes
Till autumn pluck from his hand
An hour-glass that holds not a sand;
From the maze that a flower-belt encloses
To the stones and sea-grass on the strand
How red was the reign of the roses
Over the rose-crowned land!

The year of the rose is brief;
From the first blade blown to the sheaf,
From the thin green leaf to the gold,
It has time to be sweet and grow old,

To triumph and leave not a leaf
For witness in winter's sight
How lovers once in the light
Would mix their breath with its breath,
And its spirit was quenched not of night,
As love is subdued not of death.

In the red-rose land not a mile
Of the meadows from stile to stile,
Of the valleys from stream to stream,
But the air was a long sweet dream
And the earth was a sweet wide smile
Red-mouthed of a goddess, returned
From the sea which had borne her and burned,
That with one swift smile of her mouth
Looked full on the north as it yearned,
And the north was more than the south.

For the north, when winter was long,
In his heart had made him a song,
And clothed it with wings of desire,
And shod it with shoon as of fire,
To carry the tale of his wrong
To the south-west wind by the sea.
That none might bear it but he
To the ear of the goddess unknown
Who waits till her time shall be
To take the world for a throne.

In the earth beneath, and above
In the heaven where her name is love,
She warms with light from her eyes
The seasons of life as they rise,
And her eyes are as eyes of a dove,
But the wings that lift her and bear
As an eagle's, and all her hair
As fire by the wind's breath curled,
And her passage is song through the air,
And her presence is spring through the world.

So turned she northward and came,
And the white-thorn land was aflame
With the fires that were shed from her feet,
That the north, by her love made sweet,
Should be called by a rose-red name;
And a murmur was heard as of doves,
And a music beginning of loves
In the light that the roses made,

Such light as the music loves,
The music of man with maid.

But the days drop one upon one,
And a chill soft wind is begun
In the heart of the rose-red maze
That weeps for the roseleaf days
And the reign of the rose undone
That ruled so long in the light,
And by spirit, and not by sight,
Through the darkness thrilled with its breath,
Still ruled in the viewless night,
As love might rule over death.

The time of lovers is brief;
From the fair first joy to the grief
That tells when love is grown old,
From the warm wild kiss to the cold,
From the red to the white-rose leaf,
They have but a season to seem
As roseleaves lost on a stream
That part not and pass not apart
As a spirit from dream to dream,
As a sorrow from heart to heart.

From the bloom and the gloom that encloses
The death-bed of Love where he dozes
Till a relic be left not of sand
To the hour-glass that breaks in his hand;
From the change in the grey garden-closes
To the last stray grass of the strand,
A rain and ruin of roses
Over the red-rose land

A WASTED VIGIL

I

Couldst thou not watch with me one hour? Behold,
Dawn skims the sea with flying feet of gold,
With sudden feet that graze the gradual sea;
Couldst thou not watch with me?

II

What, not one hour? for star by star the night
Falls, and her thousands world by world take flight;
They die, and day survives, and what of thee?
Couldst thou not watch with me?

III

Lo, far in heaven the web of night undone,
And on the sudden sea the gradual sun;
Wave to wave answers, tree responds to tree;
Couldst thou not watch with me?

IV

Sunbeam by sunbeam creeps from line to line,
Foam by foam quickens on the brightening brine;
Sail by sail passes, flower by flower gets free;
Couldst thou not watch with me?

V

Last year, a brief while since, an age ago,
A whole year past, with bud and bloom and snow,
O moon that wast in heaven, what friends were we!
Couldst thou not watch with me?

VI

Old moons, and last year's flowers, and last year's snows!
Who now saith to thee, moon? or who saith, rose?
O dust and ashes, once found fair to see!
Couldst thou not watch with me?

VII

O dust and ashes, once thought sweet to smell!
With me it is not, is it with thee well?
O sea-drift blown from windward back to lee!
Couldst thou not watch with me?

VIII

The old year's dead hands are full of their dead flowers.
The old days are full of dead old loves of ours,
Born as a rose, and briefer born than she;
Couldst thou not watch with me?

IX

Could two days live again of that dead year,
One would say, seeking us and passing here,
Where is she? and one answering, Where is he?
Couldst thou not watch with me?

X

Nay, those two lovers are not anywhere;
If we were they, none knows us what we were,
Nor aught of all their barren grief and glee.
Couldst thou not watch with me?

XI

Half false, half fair, all feeble, be my verse
Upon thee not for blessing nor for curse;
For some must stand, and some must fall or flee;
Couldst thou not watch with me?

XII

As a new moon above spent stars thou wast;
But stars endure after the moon is past.
Couldst thou not watch one hour, though I watch three?
Couldst thou not watch with me?

XIII

What of the night? The night is full, the tide
Storms inland, the most ancient rocks divide;
Yet some endure, and bow nor head nor knee;
Couldst thou not watch with me?

XIV

Since thou art not as these are, go thy ways;
Thou hast no part in all my nights and days.
Lie still, sleep on, be glad—as such things be;
Thou couldst not watch with me.

THE COMPLAINT OF LISA

(Double Sestina)

Decameron, x. 7

There is no woman living that draws breath
So sad as I, though all things sadden her.
There is not one upon life's weariest way
Who is weary as I am weary of all but death.
Toward whom I look as looks the sunflower
All day with all his whole soul toward the sun;
While in the sun's sight I make moan all day,
And all night on my sleepless maiden bed
Weep and call out on death, O Love, and thee,
That thou or he would take me to the dead,
And know not what thing evil I have done
That life should lay such heavy hand on me.

Alas, Love, what is this thou wouldst with me?
What honour shall thou have to quench my breath,
Or what shall my heart broken profit thee?
O Love, O great god Love, what have I done,
That thou shouldst hunger so after my death?
My heart is harmless as my life's first day:
Seek out some false fair woman, and plague her
Till her tears even as my tears fill her bed:
I am the least flower in thy flowery way,
But till my time be come that I be dead
Let me live out my flower-time in the sun
Though my leaves shut before the sunflower.

O Love, Love, Love, the kingly sunflower!
Shall he the sun hath looked on look on me,
That live down here in shade, out of the sun,
Here living in the sorrow and shadow of death?
Shall he that feeds his heart full of the day
Care to give mine eyes light, or my lips breath?
Because she loves him shall my lord love her
Who is as a worm in my lord's kingly way?
I shall not see him or know him alive or dead;

But thou, I know thee, O Love, and pray to thee
That in brief while my brief life-days be done,
And the worm quickly make my marriage-bed.

For underground there is no sleepless bed:
But here since I beheld my sunflower
These eyes have slept not, seeing all night and day
His sunlike eyes, and face fronting the sun.
Wherefore if anywhere be any death,
I would fain find and fold him fast to me,
That I may sleep with the world's eldest dead,
With her that died seven centuries since, and her
That went last night down the night-wandering way.
For this is sleep indeed, when labour is done,
Without love, without dreams, and without breath,
And without thought, O name unnamed! of thee.

Ah, but, forgetting all things, shall I thee?
Wilt thou not be as now about my bed
There underground as here before the sun?
Shall not thy vision vex me alive and dead,
Thy moving vision without form or breath?
I read long since the bitter tale of her
Who read the tale of Launcelot on a day,
And died, and had no quiet after death,
But was moved ever along a weary way,
Lost with her love in the underworld; ah me,
O my king, O my lordly sunflower,
Would God to me too such a thing were done!

But if such sweet and bitter things be done,
Then, flying from life, I shall not fly from thee.
For in that living world without a sun
Thy vision will lay hold upon me dead,
And meet and mock me, and mar my peace in death.
Yet if being wroth God had such pity on her,
Who was a sinner and foolish in her day,
That even in hell they twain should breathe one breath,
Why should he not in some wise pity me?
So if I sleep not in my soft strait bed
I may look up and see my sunflower
As he the sun, in some divine strange way.

O poor my heart, well knowest thou in what way
This sore sweet evil unto us was done.
For on a holy and a heavy day
I was arisen out of my still small bed
To see the knights tilt, and one said to me

"The king," and seeing him, somewhat stopped my breath,
And if the girl spake more, I heard not her,
For only I saw what I shall see when dead,
A kingly flower of knights, a sunflower,
That shone against the sunlight like the sun,
And like a fire, O heart, consuming thee,
The fire of love that lights the pyre of death.

Howbeit I shall not die an evil death
Who have loved in such a sad and sinless way,
That this my love, lord, was no shame to thee.
So when mine eyes are shut against the sun,
O my soul's sun, O the world's sunflower,
Thou nor no man will quite despise me dead.
And dying I pray with all my low last breath
That thy whole life may be as was that day,
That feast-day that made trothplight death and me,
Giving the world light of thy great deeds done;
And that fair face brightening thy bridal bed,
That God be good as God hath been to her.

That all things goodly and glad remain with her,
All things that make glad life and goodly death;
That as a bee sucks from a sunflower
Honey, when summer draws delighted breath,
Her soul may drink of thy soul in like way,
And love make life a fruitful marriage-bed
Where day may bring forth fruits of joy to day
And night to night till days and nights be dead.
And as she gives light of her love to thee,
Give thou to her the old glory of days long done;
And either give some heat of light to me,
To warm me where I sleep without the sun.

O sunflower made drunken with the sun,
O knight whose lady's heart draws thine to her,
Great king, glad lover, I have a word to thee.
There is a weed lives out of the sun's way,
Hid from the heat deep in the meadow's bed,
That swoons and whitens at the wind's least breath,
A flower star-shaped, that all a summer day
Will gaze her soul out on the sunflower
For very love till twilight finds her dead.
But the great sunflower heeds not her poor death,
Knows not when all her loving life is done;
And so much knows my lord the king of me.

Aye, all day long he has no eye for me;

With golden eye following the golden sun
From rose-coloured to purple-pillowed bed,
From birthplace to the flame-lit place of death,
From eastern end to western of his way.
So mine eye follows thee, my sunflower,
So the white star-flower turns and yearns to thee,
The sick weak weed, not well alive or dead,
Trod underfoot if any pass by her,
Pale, without colour of summer or summer breath
In the shrunk shuddering petals, that have done
No work but love, and die before the day.

But thou, to-day, to-morrow, and every day,
Be glad and great, O love whose love slays me.
Thy fervent flower made fruitful from the sun
Shall drop its golden seed in the world's way,
That all men thereof nourished shall praise thee
For grain and flower and fruit of works well done;
Till thy shed seed, O shining sunflower,
Bring forth such growth of the world's garden-bed
As like the sun shall outlive age and death.
And yet I would thine heart had heed of her
Who loves thee alive; but not till she be dead.
Come, Love, then, quickly, and take her utmost breath.

Song, speak for me who am dumb as are the dead;
From my sad bed of tears I send forth thee,
To fly all day from sun's birth to sun's death
Down the sun's way after the flying sun,
For love of her that gave thee wings and breath,
Ere day be done, to seek the sunflower.

FOR THE FEAST OF GIORDANO BRUNO, PHILOSOPHER AND MARTYR

I

Son of the lightning and the light that glows
Beyond the lightning's or the morning's light,
Soul splendid with all-righteous love of right,
In whose keen fire all hopes and fears and woes
Were clean consumed, and from their ashes rose
Transfigured, and intolerable to sight
Save of purged eyes whose lids had cast off night,
In love's and wisdom's likeness when they close,
Embracing, and between them truth stands fast,
Embraced of either; thou whose feet were set

On English earth while this was England yet,
Our friend that art, our Sidney's friend that wast,
Heart hardier found and higher than all men's past,
Shall we not praise thee though thine own forget?

II

Lift up thy light on us and on thine own,
O soul whose spirit on earth was as a rod
To scourge off priests, a sword to pierce their God,
A staff for man's free thought to walk alone,
A lamp to lead him far from shrine and throne
On ways untrodden where his fathers trod
Ere earth's heart withered at a high priest's nod
And all men's mouths that made not prayer made moan.
From bonds and torments and the ravening flame
Surely thy spirit of sense rose up to greet
Lucretius, where such only spirits meet,
And walk with him apart till Shelley came
To make the heaven of heavens more heavenly sweet
And mix with yours a third incorporate name.

AVE ATQUE VALE

IN MEMORY OF CHARLES BAUDELAIRE

Nous devrions pourtant lui porter quelques fleurs;
Les morts, les pauvres morts, ont de grandes douleurs,
Et quand Octobre souffle, émondeur des vieux arbres,
Son vent mélancolique à l'entour de leurs marbres,
Certe, ils doivent trouver les vivants bien ingrats.
Les Fleurs du Mal.

I

Shall I strew on thee rose or rue or laurel,
Brother, on this that was the veil of thee?
Or quiet sea-flower moulded by the sea,
Or simplest growth of meadow-sweet or sorrel,
Such as the summer-sleepy Dryads weave,
Waked up by snow-soft sudden rains at eve?
Or wilt thou rather, as on earth before,
Half-faded fiery blossoms, pale with heat
And full of bitter summer, but more sweet

To thee than gleanings of a northern shore
Trod by no tropic feet?

II

For always thee the fervid languid glories
Allured of heavier suns in mightier skies;
Thine ears knew all the wandering watery sighs
Where the sea sobs round Lesbian promontories,
The barren kiss of piteous wave to wave
That knows not where is that Leucadian grave
Which hides too deep the supreme head of song.
Ah, salt and sterile as her kisses were,
The wild sea winds her and the green gulfs bear
Hither and thither, and vex and work her wrong,
Blind gods that cannot spare.

III

Thou sawest, in thine old singing season, brother,
Secrets and sorrows unbeheld of us:
Fierce loves, and lovely leaf-buds poisonous,
Bare to thy subtler eye, but for none other
Blowing by night in some unbreathed-in clime;
The hidden harvest of luxurious time,
Sin without shape, and pleasure without speech;
And where strange dreams in a tumultuous sleep
Make the shut eyes of stricken spirits weep;
And with each face thou sawest the shadow on each,
Seeing as men sow men reap.

IV

O sleepless heart and sombre soul unsleeping,
That were athirst for sleep and no more life
And no more love, for peace and no more strife!
Now the dim gods of death have in their keeping
Spirit and body and all the springs of song,
Is it well now where love can do no wrong,
Where stingless pleasure has no foam or fang
Behind the unopening closure of her lips?
Is it not well where soul from body slips
And flesh from bone divides without a pang
As dew from flower-bell drips?

V

It is enough; the end and the beginning
Are one thing to thee, who art past the end.
O hand unclasped of unbeholden friend,
For thee no fruits to pluck, no palms for winning,
No triumph and no labour and no lust,
Only dead yew-leaves and a little dust.
O quiet eyes wherein the light saith nought,
Whereto the day is dumb, nor any night
With obscure finger silences your sight,
Nor in your speech the sudden soul speaks thought,
Sleep, and have sleep for light.

VI

Now all strange hours and all strange loves are over,
Dreams and desires and sombre songs and sweet,
Hast thou found place at the great knees and feet
Of some pale Titan-woman like a lover,
Such as thy vision here solicited,
Under the shadow of her fair vast head,
The deep division of prodigious breasts,
The solemn slope of mighty limbs asleep,
The weight of awful tresses that still keep
The savour and shade of old-world pine-forests
Where the wet hill-winds weep?

VII

Hast thou found any likeness for thy vision?
O gardener of strange flowers, what bud, what bloom,
Hast thou found sown, what gathered in the gloom?
What of despair, of rapture, of derision,
What of life is there, what of ill or good?
Are the fruits grey like dust or bright like blood?
Does the dim ground grow any seed of ours,
The faint fields quicken any terrene root,
In low lands where the sun and moon are mute
And all the stars keep silence? Are there flowers
At all, or any fruit?

VIII

Alas, but though my flying song flies after,
O sweet strange elder singer, thy more fleet
Singing, and footprints of thy fleeter feet,
Some dim derision of mysterious laughter
From the blind tongueless warders of the dead,
Some gainless glimpse of Proserpine's veiled head,
Some little sound of unregarded tears
Wept by effaced unprofitable eyes,
And from pale mouths some cadence of dead sighs—
These only, these the hearkening spirit hears,
Sees only such things rise.

IX

Thou art far too far for wings of words to follow,
Far too far off for thought or any prayer.
What ails us with thee, who art wind and air?
What ails us gazing where all seen is hollow?
Yet with some fancy, yet with some desire,
Dreams pursue death as winds a flying fire,
Our dreams pursue our dead and do not find.
Still, and more swift than they, the thin flame flies,
The low light fails us in elusive skies,
Still the foiled earnest ear is deaf, and blind
Are still the eluded eyes.

X

Not thee, O never thee, in all time's changes,
Not thee, but this the sound of thy sad soul,
The shadow of thy swift spirit, this shut scroll
I lay my hand on, and not death estranges
My spirit from communion of thy song—
These memories and these melodies that throng
Veiled porches of a Muse funereal—
These I salute, these touch, these clasp and fold
As though a hand were in my hand to hold,
Or through mine ears a mourning musical
Of many mourners rolled.

XI

I among these, I also, in such station
As when the pyre was charred, and piled the sods,
And offering to the dead made, and their gods,

The old mourners had, standing to make libation,
I stand, and to the gods and to the dead
Do reverence without prayer or praise, and shed
Offering to these unknown, the gods of gloom,
And what of honey and spice my seedlands bear,
And what I may of fruits in this chilled air,
And lay, Orestes-like, across the tomb
A curl of severed hair.

XII

But by no hand nor any treason stricken,
Not like the low-lying head of Him, the King,
The flame that made of Troy a ruinous thing,
Thou liest, and on this dust no tears could quicken
There fall no tears like theirs that all men hear
Fall tear by sweet imperishable tear
Down the opening leaves of holy poets' pages.
Thee not Orestes, not Electra mourns;
But bending us-ward with memorial urns
The most high Muses that fulfil all ages
Weep, and our God's heart yearns.

XIII

For, sparing of his sacred strength, not often
Among us darkling here the lord of light
Makes manifest his music and his might
In hearts that open and in lips that soften
With the soft flame and heat of songs that shine.
Thy lips indeed he touched with bitter wine,
And nourished them indeed with bitter bread;
Yet surely from his hand thy soul's food came,
The fire that scarred thy spirit at his flame
Was lighted, and thine hungering heart he fed
Who feeds our hearts with fame.

XIV

Therefore he too now at thy soul's sunsetting,
God of all suns and songs, he too bends down
To mix his laurel with thy cypress crown,
And save thy dust from blame and from forgetting.
Therefore he too, seeing all thou wert and art,
Compassionate, with sad and sacred heart,

Mourns thee of many his children the last dead,
And hallows with strange tears and alien sighs
Thine unmelodious mouth and sunless eyes,
And over thine irrevocable head
Sheds light from the under skies.

XV

And one weeps with him in the ways Lethean,
And stains with tears her changing bosom chill:
That obscure Venus of the hollow hill,
That thing transformed which was the Cytherean,
With lips that lost their Grecian laugh divine
Long since, and face no more called Erycine;
A ghost, a bitter and luxurious god.
Thee also with fair flesh and singing spell
Did she, a sad and second prey, compel
Into the footless places once more trod,
And shadows hot from hell.

XVI

And now no sacred staff shall break in blossom,
No choral salutation lure to light
A spirit sick with perfume and sweet night
And love's tired eyes and hands and barren bosom.
There is no help for these things; none to mend
And none to mar; not all our songs, O friend,
Will make death clear or make life durable.
Howbeit with rose and ivy and wild vine
And with wild notes about this dust of thine
At least I fill the place where white dreams dwell
And wreathe an unseen shrine.

XVII

Sleep; and if life was bitter to thee, pardon,
If sweet, give thanks; thou hast no more to live;
And to give thanks is good, and to forgive.
Out of the mystic and the mournful garden
Where all day through thine hands in barren braid
Wove the sick flowers of secrecy and shade,
Green buds of sorrow and sin, and remnants grey,
Sweet-smelling, pale with poison, sanguine-hearted,
Passions that sprang from sleep and thoughts that started,

Shall death not bring us all as thee one day
Among the days departed?

For thee, O now a silent soul, my brother,
Take at my hands this garland, and farewell.
Thin is the leaf, and chill the wintry smell,
And chill the solemn earth, a fatal mother,
With sadder than the Niobean womb,
And in the hollow of her breasts a tomb.
Content thee, howsoe'er, whose days are done;
There lies not any troublous thing before,
Nor sight nor sound to war against thee more,
For whom all winds are quiet as the sun,
All waters as the shore.

MEMORIAL VERSES ON THE DEATH OF THÉOPHILE GAUTIER

Death, what hast thou to do with me? So saith
Love, with eyes set against the face of Death;
What have I done, O thou strong Death, to thee,
That mine own lips should wither from thy breath?

Though thou be blind as fire or as the sea,
Why should thy waves and storms make war on me?
Is it for hate thou hast to find me fair,
Or for desire to kiss, if it might be,

My very mouth of song, and kill me there?
So with keen rains vexing his crownless hair.
With bright feet bruised from no delightful way,
Through darkness and the disenchanted air,

Lost Love went weeping half a winter's day.
And the armèd wind that smote him seemed to say,
How shall the dew live when the dawn is fled,
Or wherefore should the Mayflower outlast May?

Then Death took Love by the right hand and said,
Smiling: Come now and look upon thy dead.
But Love cast down the glories of his eyes,
And bowed down like a flower his flowerless head.

And Death spake, saying: What ails thee in such wise,

Being god, to shut thy sight up from the skies?
If thou canst see not, hast thou ears to hear?
Or is thy soul too as a leaf that dies?

Even as he spake with fleshless lips of fear,
But soft as sleep sings in a tired man's ear,
Behold, the winter was not, and its might
Fell, and fruits broke forth of the barren year.

And upon earth was largess of great light,
And moving music winged for worldwide flight,
And shapes and sounds of gods beheld and heard,
And day's foot set upon the neck of night.

And with such song the hollow ways were stirred
As of a god's heart hidden in a bird,
Or as the whole soul of the sun in spring
Should find full utterance in one flower-soft word,

And all the season should break forth and sing
From one flower's lips, in one rose triumphing;
Such breath and light of song as of a flame
Made ears and spirits of them that heard it ring.

And Love beholding knew not for the same
The shape that led him, nor in face nor name,
For he was bright and great of thews and fair,
And in Love's eyes he was not Death, but Fame.

Not that grey ghost whose life is empty and bare
And his limbs moulded out of mortal air,
A cloud of change that shifts into a shower
And dies and leaves no light for time to wear:

But a god clothed with his own joy and power,
A god re-risen out of his mortal hour
Immortal, king and lord of time and space,
With eyes that look on them as from a tower.

And where he stood the pale sepulchral place
Bloomed, as new life might in a bloodless face,
And where men sorrowing came to seek a tomb
With funeral flowers and tears for grief and grace,

They saw with light as of a world in bloom
The portal of the House of Fame illume
The ways of life wherein we toiling tread,
And watched the darkness as a brand consume.

And through the gates where rule the deathless dead
The sound of a new singer's soul was shed
That sang among his kinsfolk, and a beam
Shot from the star on a new ruler's head.

A new star lighting the Lethean stream,
A new song mixed into the song supreme
Made of all souls of singers and their might,
That makes of life and time and death a dream.

Thy star, thy song, O soul that in our sight
Wast as a sun that made for man's delight
Flowers and all fruits in season, being so near
The sun-god's face, our god that gives us light.

To him of all gods that we love or fear
Thou amongst all men by thy name wast dear,
Dear to the god that gives us spirit of song
To bind and burn all hearts of men that hear.

The god that makes men's words too sweet and strong
For life or time or death to do them wrong,
Who sealed with his thy spirit for a sign
And filled it with his breath thy whole life long.

Who made thy moist lips fiery with new wine
Pressed from the grapes of song, the sovereign vine,
And with all love of all things loveliest
Gave thy soul power to make them more divine.

That thou might'st breathe upon the breathless rest
Of marble, till the brows and lips and breast
Felt fall from off them as a cancelled curse
That speechless sleep wherewith they lived opprest.

Who gave thee strength and heat of spirit to pierce
All clouds of form and colour that disperse,
And leave the spirit of beauty to remould
In types of clean chryselephantine verse.

Who gave thee words more golden than fine gold
To carve in shapes more glorious than of old,
And build thy songs up in the sight of time
As statues set in godhead manifold:

In sight and scorn of temporal change and clime
That meet the sun re-risen with refluent rhyme

—As god to god might answer face to face—
From lips whereon the morning strikes sublime.

Dear to the god, our god who gave thee place
Among the chosen of days, the royal race,
The lords of light, whose eyes of old and ears
Saw even on earth and heard him for a space.

There are the souls of those once mortal years
That wrought with fire of joy and light of tears
In words divine as deeds that grew thereof
Such music as he swoons with love who hears.

There are the lives that lighten from above
Our under lives, the spheral souls that move
Through the ancient heaven of song-illumined air
Whence we that hear them singing die with love.

There all the crowned Hellenic heads, and there
The old gods who made men godlike as they were,
The lyric lips wherefrom all songs take fire,
Live eyes, and light of Apollonian hair.

There, round the sovereign passion of that lyre
Which the stars hear and tremble with desire,
The ninefold light Pierian is made one
That here we see divided, and aspire,

Seeing, after this or that crown to be won;
But where they hear the singing of the sun,
All form, all sound, all colour, and all thought
Are as one body and soul in unison.

There the song sung shines as a picture wrought,
The painted mouths sing that on earth say nought,
The carven limbs have sense of blood and growth
And large-eyed life that seeks nor lacks not aught.

There all the music of thy living mouth
Lives, and all loves wrought of thine hand in youth
And bound about the breasts and brows with gold
And coloured pale or dusk from north or south.

Fair living things made to thy will of old,
Born of thy lips, no births of mortal mould,
That in the world of song about thee wait
Where thought and truth are one and manifold.

Within the graven lintels of the gate
That here divides our vision and our fate,
The dreams we walk in and the truths of sleep,
All sense and spirit have life inseparate.

There what one thinks, is his to grasp and keep;
There are no dreams, but very joys to reap,
No foiled desires that die before delight,
No fears to see across our joys and weep.

There hast thou all thy will of thought and sight,
All hope for harvest, and all heaven for flight;
The sunrise of whose golden-mouthed glad head
To paler songless ghosts was heat and light.

Here where the sunset of our year is red
Men think of thee as of the summer dead,
Gone forth before the snows, before thy day,
With unshod feet, with brows unchapleted.

Couldst thou not wait till age had wound, they say,
Round those wreathed brows his soft white blossoms? Nay,
Why shouldst thou vex thy soul with this harsh air,
Thy bright-winged soul, once free to take its way?

Nor for men's reverence hadst thou need to wear
The holy flower of grey time-hallowed hair;
Nor were it fit that aught of thee grew old,
Fair lover all thy days of all things fair.

And hear we not thy words of molten gold
Singing? or is their light and heat acold
Whereat men warmed their spirits? Nay, for all
These yet are with us, ours to hear and hold.

The lovely laughter, the clear tears, the call
Of love to love on ways where shadows fall,
Through doors of dim division and disguise,
And music made of doubts unmusical;

The love that caught strange light from death's own eyes,[1]
And filled death's lips with fiery words and sighs,
And half asleep let feed from veins of his
Her close red warm snake's mouth, Egyptian-wise:

And that great night of love more strange than this,[2]
When she that made the whole world's bale and bliss
Made king of all the world's desire a slave,

And killed him in mid kingdom with a kiss;

Veiled loves that shifted shapes and shafts, and gave,[3]
Laughing, strange gifts to hands that durst not crave,
Flowers double-blossomed, fruits of scent and hue
Sweet as the bride-bed, stranger than the grave;

All joys and wonders of old lives and new
That ever in love's shine or shadow grew,
And all the grief whereof he dreams and grieves,
And all sweet roots fed on his light and dew;

All these through thee our spirit of sense perceives,
As threads in the unseen woof thy music weaves,
Birds caught and snared that fill our ears with thee,
Bay-blossoms in thy wreath of brow-bound leaves.

Mixed with the masque of death's old comedy
Though thou too pass, have here our flowers, that we
For all the flowers thou gav'st upon thee shed,
And pass not crownless to Persephone.

Blue lotus-blooms and white and rosy-red
We wind with poppies for thy silent head,
And on this margin of the sundering sea
Leave thy sweet light to rise upon the dead.

[Footnote 1: *La Morte Amoureuse.*]
[Footnote 2: *Une Nuit de Cléopâtre.*]
[Footnote 3: *Mademoiselle de Maupin.*]

SONNET

(WITH A COPY OF Mademoiselle de Maupin)

This is the golden book of spirit and sense,
The holy writ of beauty; he that wrought
Made it with dreams and faultless words and thought
That seeks and finds and loses in the dense
Dim air of life that beauty's excellence
Wherewith love makes one hour of life distraught
And all hours after follow and find not aught.
Here is that height of all love's eminence
Where man may breathe but for a breathing-space
And feel his soul burn as an altar-fire
To the unknown God of unachieved desire,

And from the middle mystery of the place
Watch lights that break, hear sounds as of a quire,
But see not twice unveiled the veiled God's face.

AGE AND SONG

(TO BARRY CORNWALL)

I

In vain men tell us time can alter
Old loves or make old memories falter,
That with the old year the old year's life closes.
The old dew still falls on the old sweet flowers,
The old sun revives the new-fledged hours,
The old summer rears the new-born roses.

II

Much more a Muse that bears upon her
Raiment and wreath and flower of honour,
Gathered long since and long since woven,
Fades not or falls as fall the vernal
Blossoms that bear no fruit eternal,
By summer or winter charred or cloven.

III

No time casts down, no time upraises,
Such loves, such memories, and such praises,
As need no grace of sun or shower,
No saving screen from frost or thunder
To tend and house around and under
The imperishable and fearless flower.

IV

Old thanks, old thoughts, old aspirations,
Outlive men's lives and lives of nations,
Dead, but for one thing which survives—
The inalienable and unpriced treasure,
The old joy of power, the old pride of pleasure,
That lives in light above men's lives.

(October 4, 1874)

I

In the garden of death, where the singers whose names are deathless
One with another make music unheard of men,
Where the dead sweet roses fade not of lips long breathless,
And the fair eyes shine that shall weep not or change again,
Who comes now crowned with the blossom of snow-white years?
What music is this that the world of the dead men hears?

II

Beloved of men, whose words on our lips were honey,
Whose name in our ears and our fathers' ears was sweet,
Like summer gone forth of the land his songs made sunny,
To the beautiful veiled bright world where the glad ghosts meet,
Child, father, bridegroom and bride, and anguish and rest,
No soul shall pass of a singer than this more blest.

III

Blest for the years' sweet sake that were filled and brightened,
As a forest with birds, with the fruit and the flower of his song;
For the souls' sake blest that heard, and their cares were lightened,
For the hearts' sake blest that have fostered his name so long;
By the living and dead lips blest that have loved his name,
And clothed with their praise and crowned with their love for fame.

IV

Ah, fair and fragrant his fame as flowers that close not,
That shrink not by day for heat or for cold by night,
As a thought in the heart shall increase when the heart's self knows not,
Shall endure in our ears as a sound, in our eyes as a light;
Shall wax with the years that wane and the seasons' chime,
As a white rose thornless that grows in the garden of time.

V

The same year calls, and one goes hence with another,
And men sit sad that were glad for their sweet songs' sake;
The same year beckons, and elder with younger brother
Takes mutely the cup from his hand that we all shall take.[1]
They pass ere the leaves be past or the snows be come;
And the birds are loud, but the lips that outsang them dumb.

VI

Time takes them home that we loved, fair names and famous,
To the soft long sleep, to the broad sweet bosom of death;
But the flower of their souls he shall take not away to shame us,
Nor the lips lack song for ever that now lack breath.
For with us shall the music and perfume that die not dwell,
Though the dead to our dead bid welcome, and we farewell.

[Footnote 1: Sydney Dobell died August 22, 1874.]

EPICEDE

(James Lorimer Graham died at Florence, April 30, 1876)

Life may give for love to death
Little; what are life's gifts worth
To the dead wrapt round with earth?
Yet from lips of living breath
Sighs or words we are fain to give,
All that yet, while yet we live,
Life may give for love to death.

Dead so long before his day,
Passed out of the Italian sun
To the dark where all is done,
Fallen upon the verge of May;
Here at life's and April's end
How should song salute my friend
Dead so long before his day?

Not a kindlier life or sweeter
Time, that lights and quenches men,
Now may quench or light again,
Mingling with the mystic metre
Woven of all men's lives with his
Not a clearer note than this,

Not a kindlier life or sweeter.

In this heavenliest part of earth
He that living loved the light,
Light and song, may rest aright,
One in death, if strange in birth,
With the deathless dead that make
Life the lovelier for their sake
In this heavenliest part of earth.

Light, and song, and sleep at last—
Struggling hands and suppliant knees
Get no goodlier gift than these.
Song that holds remembrance fast,
Light that lightens death, attend
Round their graves who have to friend
Light, and song, and sleep at last.

TO VICTOR HUGO

He had no children, who for love of men,
Being God, endured of Gods such things as thou,
Father; nor on his thunder-beaten brow
Fell such a woe as bows thine head again,
Twice bowed before, though godlike, in man's ken,
And seen too high for any stroke to bow
Save this of some strange God's that bends it now
The third time with such weight as bruised it then.
Fain would grief speak, fain utter for love's sake
Some word; but comfort who might bid thee take?
What God in your own tongue shall talk with thee,
Showing how all souls that look upon the sun
Shall be for thee one spirit and thy son,
And thy soul's child the soul of man to be?

January 3, 1876.

INFERIAE

Spring, and the light and sound of things on earth
Requickening, all within our green sea's girth;
A time of passage or a time of birth
Fourscore years since as this year, first and last.

The sun is all about the world we see,
The breath and strength of very spring; and we
Live, love, and feed on our own hearts; but he
Whose heart fed mine has passed into the past.

Past, all things born with sense and blood and breath;
The flesh hears nought that now the spirit saith.
If death be like as birth and birth as death,
The first was fair—more fair should be the last.

Fourscore years since, and come but one month more
The count were perfect of his mortal score
Whose sail went seaward yesterday from shore
To cross the last of many an unsailed sea.

Light, love and labour up to life's last height,
These three were stars unsetting in his sight;
Even as the sun is life and heat and light
And sets not nor is dark when dark are we.

The life, the spirit, and the work were one
That here—ah, who shall say, that here are done?
Not I, that know not; father, not thy son,
For all the darkness of the night and sea.

March 5, 1877

A BIRTH-SONG

(For Olivia Frances Madox Rossetti, born September 20, 1875)

Out of the dark sweet sleep
Where no dreams laugh or weep
Borne through bright gates of birth
Into the dim sweet light
Where day still dreams of night
While heaven takes form on earth,
White rose of spirit and flesh, red lily of love,
What note of song have we
Fit for the birds and thee,
Fair nestling couched beneath the mother-dove?

Nay, in some more divine
Small speechless song of thine
Some news too good for words,
Heart-hushed and smiling, we

Might hope to have of thee,
The youngest of God's birds,
If thy sweet sense might mix itself with ours,
If ours might understand
The language of thy land,
Ere thine become the tongue of mortal hours:

Ere thy lips learn too soon
Their soft first human tune,
Sweet, but less sweet than now,
And thy raised eyes to read
Glad and good things indeed,
But none so sweet as thou:
Ere thought lift up their flower-soft lids to see
What life and love on earth
Bring thee for gifts at birth,
But none so good as thine who hast given us thee:

Now, ere thy sense forget
The heaven that fills it yet,
Now, sleeping or awake,
If thou couldst tell, or we
Ask and be heard of thee,
For love's undying sake,
From thy dumb lips divine and bright mute speech
Such news might touch our ear
That then would burn to hear
Too high a message now for man's to reach.

Ere the gold hair of corn
Had withered wast thou born,
To make the good time glad;
The time that but last year
Fell colder than a tear
On hearts and hopes turned sad,
High hopes and hearts requickening in thy dawn,
Even theirs whose life-springs, child,
Filled thine with life and smiled,
But then wept blood for half their own withdrawn.[1]

If death and birth be one,
And set with rise of sun,
And truth with dreams divine,
Some word might come with thee
From over the still sea
Deep hid in shade or shine,
Crossed by the crossing sails of death and birth,
Word of some sweet new thing

Fit for such lips to bring,
Some word of love, some afterthought of earth.

If love be strong as death,
By what so natural breath
As thine could this be said?
By what so lovely way
Could love send word to say
He lives and is not dead?
Such word alone were fit for only thee,
If his and thine have met
Where spirits rise and set,
His whom we see not, thine whom scarce we see:

His there new-born, as thou
New-born among us now;
His, here so fruitful-souled,
Now veiled and silent here,
Now dumb as thou last year,
A ghost of one year old:
If lights that change their sphere in changing meet,
Some ray might his not give
To thine who wast to live,
And make thy present with his past life sweet?

Let dreams that laugh or weep,
All glad and sad dreams, sleep;
Truth more than dreams is dear.
Let thoughts that change and fly,
Sweet thoughts and swift, go by;
More than all thought is here.
More than all hope can forge or memory feign
The life that in our eyes,
Made out of love's life, lies,
And flower-like fed with love for sun and rain.

Twice royal in its root
The sweet small olive-shoot
Here set in sacred earth;
Twice dowered with glorious grace
From either heaven-born race
First blended in its birth;
Fair God or Genius of so fair an hour,
For love of either name
Twice crowned, with love and fame,
Guard and be gracious to the fair-named flower.

October 19, 1875.

EX-VOTO

When their last hour shall rise
Pale on these mortal eyes,
Herself like one that dies,
And kiss me dying
The cold last kiss, and fold
Close round my limbs her cold
Soft shade as raiment rolled
And leave them lying,

If aught my soul would say
Might move to hear me pray
The birth-god of my day
That he might hearken,
This grace my heart should crave,
To find no landward grave
That worldly springs make brave,
World's winters darken,

Nor grow through gradual hours
The cold blind seed of flowers
Made by new beams and showers
From limbs that moulder,
Nor take my part with earth,
But find for death's new birth
A bed of larger girth,
More chaste and colder.

Not earth's for spring and fall,
Not earth's at heart, not all
Earth's making, though men call
Earth only mother,
Not hers at heart she bare
Me, but thy child, O fair
Sea, and thy brother's care,
The wind thy brother.

Yours was I born, and ye,
The sea-wind and the sea,
Made all my soul in me
A song for ever,
A harp to string and smite

For love's sake of the bright
Wind and the sea's delight,
To fail them never:

Not while on this side death
I hear what either saith
And drink of either's breath
With heart's thanksgiving
That in my veins like wine
Some sharp salt blood of thine,
Some springtide pulse of brine,
Yet leaps up living.

When thy salt lips wellnigh
Sucked in my mouth's last sigh,
Grudged I so much to die
This death as others?
Was it no ease to think
The chalice from whose brink
Fate gave me death to drink
Was thine—my mother's?

Thee too, the all-fostering earth,
Fair as thy fairest birth,
More than thy worthiest worth,
We call, we know thee,
More sweet and just and dread
Than live men highest of head
Or even thy holiest dead
Laid low below thee.

The sunbeam on the sheaf,
The dewfall on the leaf,
All joy, all grace, all grief,
Are thine for giving;
Of thee our loves are born,
Our lives and loves, that mourn
And triumph; tares with corn,
Dead seed with living:

All good and ill things done
In eyeshot of the sun
At last in thee made one
Rest well contented;
All words of all man's breath
And works he doth or saith,
All wholly done to death,
None long lamented.

A slave to sons of thee,
Thou, seeming, yet art free;
But who shall make the sea
Serve even in seeming?
What plough shall bid it bear
Seed to the sun and the air,
Fruit for thy strong sons' fare,
Fresh wine's foam streaming?

What oldworld son of thine,
Made drunk with death as wine,
Hath drunk the bright sea's brine
With lips of laughter?
Thy blood they drink; but he
Who hath drunken of the sea
Once deeplier than of thee
Shall drink not after.

Of thee thy sons of men
Drink deep, and thirst again;
For wine in feasts, and then
In fields for slaughter;
But thirst shall touch not him
Who hath felt with sense grown dim
Rise, covering lip and limb,
The wan sea's water.

All fire of thirst that aches
The salt sea cools and slakes
More than all springs or lakes,
Freshets or shallows;
Wells where no beam can burn
Through frondage of the fern
That hides from hart and hern
The haunt it hallows.

Peace with all graves on earth
For death or sleep or birth
Be alway, one in worth
One with another;
But when my time shall be,
O mother, O my sea,
Alive or dead, take me,
Me too, my mother.

A BALLAD OF DREAMLAND

I hid my heart in a nest of roses,
Out of the sun's way, hidden apart;
In a softer bed than the soft white snow's is,
Under the roses I hid my heart.
Why would it sleep not? why should it start,
When never a leaf of the rose-tree stirred?
What made sleep flutter his wings and part?
Only the song of a secret bird.

Lie still, I said, for the wind's wing closes,
And mild leaves muffle the keen sun's dart;
Lie still, for the wind on the warm sea dozes,
And the wind is unquieter yet than thou art.
Does a thought in thee still as a thorn's wound smart?
Does the fang still fret thee of hope deferred?
What bids the lids of thy sleep dispart?
Only the song of a secret bird.

The green land's name that a charm encloses,
It never was writ in the traveller's chart,
And sweet on its trees as the fruit that grows is,
It never was sold in the merchant's mart.
The swallows of dreams through its dim fields dart,
And sleep's are the tunes in its tree-tops heard;
No hound's note wakens the wildwood hart,
Only the song of a secret bird.

ENVOI

In the world of dreams I have chosen my part,
To sleep for a season and hear no word
Of true love's truth or of light love's art,
Only the song of a secret bird.

CYRIL TOURNEUR

A sea that heaves with horror of the night,
As maddened by the moon that hangs aghast
With strain and torment of the ravening blast,
Haggard as hell, a bleak blind bloody light;
No shore but one red reef of rock in sight,
Whereon the waifs of many a wreck were cast
And shattered in the fierce nights overpast

Wherein more souls toward hell than heaven took flight;
And 'twixt the shark-toothed rocks and swallowing shoals
A cry as out of hell from all these souls
Sent through the sheer gorge of the slaughtering sea,
Whose thousand throats, full-fed with life by death,
Fill the black air with foam and furious breath;
And over all these one star—Chastity.

A BALLAD OF FRANÇOIS VILLON

PRINCE OF ALL BALLAD-MAKERS

Bird of the bitter bright grey golden morn
Scarce risen upon the dusk of dolorous years,
First of us all and sweetest singer born
Whose far shrill note the world of new men hears
Cleave the cold shuddering shade as twilight clears;
When song new-born put off the old world's attire
And felt its tune on her changed lips expire,
Writ foremost on the roll of them that came
Fresh girt for service of the latter lyre,
Villon, our sad bad glad mad brother's name!

Alas the joy, the sorrow, and the scorn,
That clothed thy life with hopes and sins and fears,
And gave thee stones for bread and tares for corn
And plume-plucked gaol-birds for thy starveling peers
Till death clipt close their flight with shameful shears;
Till shifts came short and loves were hard to hire,
When lilt of song nor twitch of twangling wire
Could buy thee bread or kisses; when light fame
Spurned like a ball and haled through brake and briar,
Villon, our sad bad glad mad brother's name!

Poor splendid wings so frayed and soiled and torn!
Poor kind wild eyes so dashed with light quick tears!
Poor perfect voice, most blithe when most forlorn,
That rings athwart the sea whence no man steers
Like joy-bells crossed with death-bells in our ears!
What far delight has cooled the fierce desire
That like some ravenous bird was strong to tire
On that frail flesh and soul consumed with flame,
But left more sweet than roses to respire,
Villon, our sad bad glad mad brother's name?

ENVOI

Prince of sweet songs made out of tears and fire,
A harlot was thy nurse, a God thy sire;
Shame soiled thy song, and song assoiled thy shame.
But from thy feet now death has washed the mire,
Love reads out first at head of all our quire,
Villon, our sad bad glad mad brother's name.

PASTICHE

Now the days are all gone over
Of our singing, love by lover,
Days of summer-coloured seas
Blown adrift through beam and breeze.

Now the nights are all past over
Of our dreaming, dreams that hover
In a mist of fair false things,
Nights afloat on wide wan wings.

Now the loves with faith for mother,
Now the fears with hope for brother,
Scarce are with us as strange words,
Notes from songs of last year's birds.

Now all good that comes or goes is
As the smell of last year's roses,
As the radiance in our eyes
Shot from summer's ere he dies.

Now the morning faintlier risen
Seems no God come forth of prison,
But a bird of plume-plucked wing,
Pale with thoughts of evening.

Now hath hope, outraced in running,
Given the torch up of his cunning
And the palm he thought to wear
Even to his own strong child—despair.

BEFORE SUNSET

In the lower lands of day

On the hither side of night,
There is nothing that will stay,
There are all things soft to sight;
Lighted shade and shadowy light
In the wayside and the way,
Hours the sun has spared to smite,
Flowers the rain has left to play.

Shall these hours run down and say
No good thing of thee and me?
Time that made us and will slay
Laughs at love in me and thee;
But if here the flowers may see
One whole hour of amorous breath,
Time shall die, and love shall be
Lord as time was over death.

SONG

Love laid his sleepless head
On a thorny rosy bed;
And his eyes with tears were red,
And pale his lips as the dead.

And fear and sorrow and scorn
Kept watch by his head forlorn,
Till the night was overworn
And the world was merry with morn.

And Joy came up with the day
And kissed Love's lips as he lay,
And the watchers ghostly and grey
Sped from his pillow away.

And his eyes as the dawn grew bright,
And his lips waxed ruddy as light:
Sorrow may reign for a night,
But day shall bring back delight.

A VISION OF SPRING IN WINTER

I

O tender time that love thinks long to see,

Sweet foot of spring that with her footfall sows
Late snowlike flowery leavings of the snows,
Be not too long irresolute to be;
O mother-month, where have they hidden thee?
Out of the pale time of the flowerless rose
I reach my heart out toward the springtime lands,
I stretch my spirit forth to the fair hours,
The purplest of the prime;
I lean my soul down over them, with hands
Made wide to take the ghostly growths of flowers;
I send my love back to the lovely time.

II

Where has the greenwood hid thy gracious head?
Veiled with what visions while the grey world grieves,
Or muffled with what shadows of green leaves,
What warm intangible green shadows spread
To sweeten the sweet twilight for thy bed?
What sleep enchants thee? what delight deceives?
Where the deep dreamlike dew before the dawn
Feels not the fingers of the sunlight yet
Its silver web unweave,
Thy footless ghost on some unfooted lawn
Whose air the unrisen sunbeams fear to fret
Lives a ghost's life of daylong dawn and eve.

III

Sunrise it sees not, neither set of star,
Large nightfall, nor imperial plenilune,
Nor strong sweet shape of the full-breasted noon;
But where the silver-sandalled shadows are,
Too soft for arrows of the sun to mar,
Moves with the mild gait of an ungrown moon:
Hard overhead the half-lit crescent swims,
The tender-coloured night draws hardly breath,
The light is listening;
They watch the dawn of slender-shapen limbs,
Virginal, born again of doubtful death,
Chill foster-father of the weanling spring.

IV

As sweet desire of day before the day,

As dreams of love before the true love born,
From the outer edge of winter overworn
The ghost arisen of May before the May
Takes through dim air her unawakened way,
The gracious ghost of morning risen ere morn.
With little unblown breasts and child-eyed looks
Following, the very maid, the girl-child spring,
Lifts windward her bright brows,
Dips her light feet in warm and moving brooks,
And kindles with her own mouth's colouring
The fearful firstlings of the plumeless boughs.

V

I seek thee sleeping, and awhile I see,
Fair face that art not, how thy maiden breath
Shall put at last the deadly days to death
And fill the fields and fire the woods with thee
And seaward hollows where my feet would be
When heaven shall hear the word that April saith
To change the cold heart of the weary time,
To stir and soften all the time to tears,
Tears joyfuller than mirth;
As even to May's clear height the young days climb
With feet not swifter than those fair first years
Whose flowers revive not with thy flowers on earth.

VI

I would not bid thee, though I might, give back
One good thing youth has given and borne away;
I crave not any comfort of the day
That is not, nor on time's retrodden track
Would turn to meet the white-robed hours or black
That long since left me on their mortal way;
Nor light nor love that has been, nor the breath
That comes with morning from the sun to be
And sets light hope on fire;
No fruit, no flower thought once too fair for death,
No flower nor hour once fallen from life's green tree,
No leaf once plucked or once fulfilled desire.

VII

The morning song beneath the stars that fled

With twilight through the moonless mountain air,
While youth with burning lips and wreathless hair
Sang toward the sun that was to crown his head,
Rising; the hopes that triumphed and fell dead,
The sweet swift eyes and songs of hours that were;
These may'st thou not give back for ever; these,
As at the sea's heart all her wrecks lie waste,
Lie deeper than the sea;
But flowers thou may'st, and winds, and hours of ease,
And all its April to the world thou may'st
Give back, and half my April back to me.

CHORIAMBICS

Love, what ailed thee to leave life that was made
lovely, we thought, with love?
What sweet visions of sleep lured thee away, down
from the light above?

What strange faces of dreams, voices that called,
hands that were raised to wave,
Lured or led thee, alas, out of the sun, down to the
sunless grave?

Ah, thy luminous eyes! once was their light fed with
the fire of day;
Now their shadowy lids cover them close, hush them
and hide away.

Ah, thy snow-coloured hands! once were they chains,
mighty to bind me fast;
Now no blood in them burns, mindless of love, senseless
of passion past.

Ah, thy beautiful hair! so was it once braided for
me, for me;
Now for death is it crowned, only for death, lover
and lord of thee.

Sweet, the kisses of death set on thy lips, colder are
they than mine;
Colder surely than past kisses that love poured for
thy lips as wine.

Lov'st thou death? is his face fairer than love's,
brighter to look upon?

Seest thou light in his eyes, light by which love's
pales and is overshone?

Lo the roses of death, grey as the dust, chiller of leaf
than snow!
Why let fall from thy hand love's that were thine,
roses that loved thee so?

Large red lilies of love, sceptral and tall, lovely for
eyes to see;
Thornless blossom of love, full of the sun, fruits that
were reared for thee.

Now death's poppies alone circle thy hair, girdle thy
breasts as white;
Bloodless blossoms of death, leaves that have sprung
never against the light.

Nay then, sleep if thou wilt; love is content; what
should he do to weep?
Sweet was love to thee once; now in thine eyes
sweeter than love is sleep.

AT PARTING

For a day and a night Love sang to us, played with us,
Folded us round from the dark and the light;
And our hearts were fulfilled of the music he made with us,
Made with our hearts and our lips while he stayed with us,
Stayed in mid passage his pinions from flight
For a day and a night.

From his foes that kept watch with his wings had he hidden us,
Covered us close from the eyes that would smite,
From the feet that had tracked and the tongues that had chidden us
Sheltering in shade of the myrtles forbidden us
Spirit and flesh growing one with delight
For a day and a night.

But his wings will not rest and his feet will not stay for us:
Morning is here in the joy of its might;
With his breath has he sweetened a night and a day for us;
Now let him pass, and the myrtles make way for us;
Love can but last in us here at his height
For a day and a night.

A SONG IN SEASON

I

Thou whose beauty
Knows no duty
Due to love that moves thee never;
Thou whose mercies
Are men's curses,
And thy smile a scourge for ever;

II

Thou that givest
Death and livest
On the death of thy sweet giving;
Thou that sparest
Not nor carest
Though thy scorn leave no love living;

III

Thou whose rootless
Flower is fruitless
As the pride its heart encloses,
But thine eyes are
As May skies are,
And thy words like spoken roses;

IV

Thou whose grace is
In men's faces
Fierce and wayward as thy will is;
Thou whose peerless
Eyes are tearless,
And thy thoughts as cold sweet lilies;

V

Thou that takest
Hearts and makest

Wrecks of loves to strew behind thee,
Whom the swallow
Sure should follow,
Finding summer where we find thee;

VI

Thou that wakest
Hearts and breakest,
And thy broken hearts forgive thee,
That wilt make no
Pause and take no
Gift that love for love might give thee;

VII

Thou that bindest
Eyes and blindest,
Serving worst who served thee longest;
Thou that speakest,
And the weakest
Heart is his that was the strongest;

VIII

Take in season
Thought with reason;
Think what gifts are ours for giving;
Hear what beauty
Owes of duty
To the love that keeps it living.

IX

Dust that covers
Long dead lovers
Song blows off with breath that brightens;
At its flashes
Their white ashes
Burst in bloom that lives and lightens.

X

Had they bent not
Head or lent not
Ear to love and amorous duties,
Song had never
Saved for ever,
Love, the least of all their beauties.

XI

All the golden
Names of olden
Women yet by men's love cherished,
All our dearest
Thoughts hold nearest,
Had they loved not, all had perished.

XII

If no fruit is
Of thy beauties,
Tell me yet, since none may win them,
What and wherefore
Love should care for
Of all good things hidden in them?

XIII

Pain for profit
Comes but of it,
If the lips that lure their lover's
Hold no treasure
Past the measure
Of the lightest hour that hovers.

XIV

If they give not
Or forgive not
Gifts or thefts for grace or guerdon,
Love that misses
Fruit of kisses
Long will bear no thankless burden.

XV

If they care not
Though love were not,
If no breath of his burn through them,
Joy must borrow
Song from sorrow,
Fear teach hope the way to woo them.

XVI

Grief has measures
Soft as pleasure's,
Fear has moods that hope lies deep in,
Songs to sing him,
Dreams to bring him,
And a red-rose bed to sleep in.

XVII

Hope with fearless
Looks and tearless
Lies and laughs too near the thunder;
Fear hath sweeter
Speech and meeter
For heart's love to hide him under.

XVIII

Joy by daytime
Fills his playtime
Full of songs loud mirth takes pride in;
Night and morrow
Weave round sorrow
Thoughts as soft as sleep to hide in.

XIX

Graceless faces,
Loveless graces,
Are but motes in light that quicken,
Sands that run down
Ere the sundown,
Roseleaves dead ere autumn sicken.

XX

Fair and fruitless
Charms are bootless
Spells to ward off age's peril;
Lips that give not
Love shall live not,
Eyes that meet not eyes are sterile.

XXI

But the beauty
Bound in duty
Fast to love that falls off never
Love shall cherish
Lest it perish,
And its root bears fruit for ever.

TWO LEADERS

[Greek:
Bate domon, megaloi philotimoi
Nuktos paides apaides, hup euphroni pompa.]

I

O great and wise, clear-souled and high of heart,
One the last flower of Catholic love, that grows
Amid bare thorns their only thornless rose,
From the fierce juggling of the priests' loud mart
Yet alien, yet unspotted and apart
From the blind hard foul rout whose shameless shows
Mock the sweet heaven whose secret no man knows
With prayers and curses and the soothsayer's art;
One like a storm-god of the northern foam
Strong, wrought of rock that breasts and breaks the sea
And thunders back its thunder, rhyme for rhyme
Answering, as though to outroar the tides of time
And bid the world's wave back—what song should be
Theirs that with praise would bring and sing you home?

II

With all our hearts we praise you whom ye hate,
High souls that hate us; for our hopes are higher,
And higher than yours the goal of our desire,
Though high your ends be as your hearts are great.
Your world of Gods and kings, of shrine and state,
Was of the night when hope and fear stood nigher,
Wherein men walked by light of stars and fire
Till man by day stood equal with his fate.
Honour not hate we give you, love not fear,
Last prophets of past kind, who fill the dome
Of great dead Gods with wrath and wail, nor hear
Time's word and man's: "Go honoured hence, go home,
Night's childless children; here your hour is done;
Pass with the stars, and leave us with the sun."

VICTOR HUGO IN 1877

"Dazzle mine eyes, or do I see three suns?"

Above the spring-tide sundawn of the year,
A sunlike star, not born of day or night,
Filled the fair heaven of spring with heavenlier light,
Made of all ages orbed in one sole sphere
Whose light was as a Titan's smile or tear;
Then rose a ray more flowerlike, starry white,
Like a child's eye grown lovelier with delight,
Sweet as a child's heart-lightening laugh to hear;
And last a fire from heaven, a fiery rain
As of God's wrath on the unclean cities, fell
And lit the shuddering shades of half-seen hell
That shrank before it and were cloven in twain;
A beacon fired by lightning, whence all time
Sees red the bare black ruins of a crime.

CHILD'S SONG

What is gold worth, say,
Worth for work or play,
Worth to keep or pay,
Hide or throw away,
Hope about or fear?
What is love worth, pray?
Worth a tear?

Golden on the mould
Lie the dead leaves rolled
Of the wet woods old,
Yellow leaves and cold,
Woods without a dove;
Gold is worth but gold;
Love's worth love.

TRIADS

I

I

The word of the sun to the sky,
The word of the wind to the sea,
The word of the moon to the night,
What may it be?

II

The sense to the flower of the fly,
The sense of the bird to the tree,
The sense to the cloud of the light,
Who can tell me?

III

The song of the fields to the kye,
The song of the lime to the bee,
The song of the depth to the height,
Who knows all three?

II

I

The message of April to May
That May sends on into June
And June gives out to July
For birthday boon;

II

The delight of the dawn in the day,
The delight of the day in the noon,
The delight of a song in a sigh
That breaks the tune;

III

The secret of passing away,
The cost of the change of the moon,
None knows it with ear or with eye,
But all will soon.

III

I

The live wave's love for the shore,
The shore's for the wave as it dies,
The love of the thunder-fire
That sears the skies,

II

We shall know not though life wax hoar,
Till all life, spent into sighs,
Burn out as consumed with desire
Of death's strange eyes;

III

Till the secret be secret no more
In the light of one hour as it flies,
Be the hour as of suns that expire
Or suns that rise.

FOUR SONGS OF FOUR SEASONS

I. WINTER IN NORTHUMBERLAND

I

Outside the garden
The wet skies harden;
The gates are barred on
The summer side:
"Shut out the flower-time,
Sunbeam and shower-time;
Make way for our time,"
Wild winds have cried.
Green once and cheery,
The woods, worn weary,
Sigh as the dreary
Weak sun goes home:
A great wind grapples
The wave, and dapples
The dead green floor of the sea with foam.

II

Through fell and moorland,
And salt-sea foreland,
Our noisy norland
Resounds and rings;
Waste waves thereunder
Are blown in sunder,
And winds make thunder
With cloudwide wings;
Sea-drift makes dimmer
The beacon's glimmer;
Nor sail nor swimmer
Can try the tides;
And snowdrifts thicken
Where, when leaves quicken,
Under the heather the sundew hides.

III

Green land and red land,
Moorside and headland,
Are white as dead land,
Are all as one;
Nor honied heather,
Nor bells to gather,
Fair with fair weather
And faithful sun:

Fierce frost has eaten
All flowers that sweeten
The fells rain-beaten;
And winds their foes
Have made the snow's bed
Down in the rose-bed;
Deep in the snow's bed bury the rose.

IV

Bury her deeper
Than any sleeper;
Sweet dreams will keep her
All day, all night;
Though sleep benumb her
And time o'ercome her,
She dreams of summer,
And takes delight,
Dreaming and sleeping
In love's good keeping,
While rain is weeping
And no leaves cling;
Winds will come bringing her
Comfort, and singing her
Stories and songs and good news of the spring.

V

Draw the white curtain
Close, and be certain
She takes no hurt in
Her soft low bed;
She feels no colder,
And grows not older,
Though snows enfold her
From foot to head;
She turns not chilly
Like weed and lily
In marsh or hilly
High watershed,
Or green soft island
In lakes of highland;
She sleeps awhile, and she is not dead.

VI

For all the hours,
Come sun, come showers,
Are friends of flowers,
And fairies all;
When frost entrapped her,
They came and lapped her
In leaves, and wrapped her
With shroud and pall;
In red leaves wound her,
With dead leaves bound her
Dead brows, and round her
A death-knell rang;
Rang the death-bell for her,
Sang, "is it well for her,
Well, is it well with you, rose?" they sang.

VII

O what and where is
The rose now, fairies,
So shrill the air is,
So wild the sky?
Poor last of roses,
Her worst of woes is
The noise she knows is
The winter's cry;
His hunting hollo
Has scared the swallow;
Fain would she follow
And fain would fly:
But wind unsettles
Her poor last petals;
Had she but wings, and she would not die.

VIII

Come, as you love her,
Come close and cover
Her white face over,
And forth again
Ere sunset glances
On foam that dances,
Through lowering lances
Of bright white rain;
And make your playtime

Of winter's daytime,
As if the Maytime
Were here to sing;
As if the snowballs
Were soft like blowballs,
Blown in a mist from the stalk in the spring.

IX

Each reed that grows in
Our stream is frozen,
The fields it flows in
Are hard and black;
The water-fairy
Waits wise and wary
Till time shall vary
And thaws come back.
"O sister, water,"
The wind besought her,
"O twin-born daughter
Of spring with me,
Stay with me, play with me,
Take the warm way with me,
Straight for the summer and oversea."

X

But winds will vary,
And wise and wary
The patient fairy
Of water waits;
All shrunk and wizen,
In iron prison,
Till spring re-risen
Unbar the gates;
Till, as with clamour
Of axe and hammer,
Chained streams that stammer
And struggle in straits
Burst bonds that shiver,
And thaws deliver
The roaring river in stormy spates.

XI

In fierce March weather
White waves break tether,
And whirled together
At either hand,
Like weeds uplifted,
The tree-trunks rifted
In spars are drifted,
Like foam or sand,
Past swamp and sallow
And reed-beds callow,
Through pool and shallow,
To wind and lee,
Till, no more tongue-tied,
Full flood and young tide
Roar down the rapids and storm the sea.

XII

As men's cheeks faded
On shores invaded,
When shorewards waded
The lords of fight;
When churl and craven
Saw hard on haven
The wide-winged raven
At mainmast height;
When monks affrighted
To windward sighted
The birds full-flighted
Of swift sea-kings;
So earth turns paler
When Storm the sailor
Steers in with a roar in the race of his wings.

XIII

O strong sea-sailor,
Whose cheek turns paler
For wind or hail or
For fear of thee?
O far sea-farer,
O thunder-bearer,
Thy songs are rarer
Than soft songs be.
O fleet-foot stranger,
O north-sea ranger

Through days of danger
And ways of fear,
Blow thy horn here for us,
Blow the sky clear for us,
Send us the song of the sea to hear.

XIV

Roll the strong stream of it
Up, till the scream of it
Wake from a dream of it
Children that sleep,
Seamen that fare for them
Forth, with a prayer for them;
Shall not God care for them,
Angels not keep?
Spare not the surges
Thy stormy scourges;
Spare us the dirges
Of wives that weep.
Turn back the waves for us:
Dig no fresh graves for us,
Wind, in the manifold gulfs of the deep.

XV

O stout north-easter,
Sea-king, land-waster,
For all thine haste, or
Thy stormy skill,
Yet hadst thou never,
For all endeavour,
Strength to dissever
Or strength to spill,
Save of his giving
Who gave our living,
Whose hands are weaving
What ours fulfil;
Whose feet tread under
The storms and thunder;
Who made our wonder to work his will.

XVI

His years and hours,

His world's blind powers,
His stars and flowers,
His nights and days,
Sea-tide and river,
And waves that shiver,
Praise God, the giver
Of tongues to praise.
Winds in their blowing,
And fruits in growing;
Time in its going,
While time shall be;
In death and living,
With one thanksgiving,
Praise him whose hand is the strength of the sea.

II. SPRING IN TUSCANY

Rose-red lilies that bloom on the banner;
Rose-cheeked gardens that revel in spring;
Rose-mouthed acacias that laugh as they climb,
Like plumes for a queen's hand fashioned to fan her
With wind more soft than a wild dove's wing,
What do they sing in the spring of their time?

If this be the rose that the world hears singing,
Soft in the soft night, loud in the day,
Songs for the fire-flies to dance as they hear;
If that be the song of the nightingale, springing
Forth in the form of a rose in May,
What do they say of the way of the year?

What of the way of the world gone Maying,
What of the work of the buds in the bowers,
What of the will of the wind on the wall,
Fluttering the wall-flowers, sighing and playing,
Shrinking again as a bird that cowers,
Thinking of hours when the flowers have to fall?

Out of the throats of the loud birds showering,
Out of the folds where the flag-lilies leap,
Out of the mouths of the roses stirred,
Out of the herbs on the walls reflowering,
Out of the heights where the sheer snows sleep,
Out of the deep and the steep, one word.

One from the lips of the lily-flames leaping,

The glad red lilies that burn in our sight,
The great live lilies for standard and crown;
One from the steeps where the pines stand sleeping,
One from the deep land, one from the height,
One from the light and the might of the town.

The lowlands laugh with delight of the highlands,
Whence May winds feed them with balm and breath
From hills that beheld in the years behind
A shape as of one from the blest souls' islands,
Made fair by a soul too fair for death,
With eyes on the light that should smite them blind.

Vallombrosa remotely remembers,
Perchance, what still to us seems so near
That time not darkens it, change not mars,
The foot that she knew when her leaves were September's,
The face lift up to the star-blind seer,
That saw from his prison arisen his stars.

And Pisa broods on her dead, not mourning,
For love of her loveliness given them in fee;
And Prato gleams with the glad monk's gift
Whose hand was there as the hand of morning;
And Siena, set in the sand's red sea,
Lifts loftier her head than the red sand's drift.

And far to the fair south-westward lightens,
Girdled and sandalled and plumed with flowers,
At sunset over the love-lit lands,
The hill-side's crown where the wild hill brightens,
Saint Fina's town of the Beautiful Towers,
Hailing the sun with a hundred hands.

Land of us all that have loved thee dearliest,
Mother of men that were lords of man,
Whose name in the world's heart works as a spell,
My last song's light, and the star of mine earliest,
As we turn from thee, sweet, who wast ours for a span,
Fare well we may not who say farewell.

III. SUMMER IN AUVERGNE

The sundawn fills the land
Full as a feaster's hand
Fills full with bloom of bland
Bright wine his cup;

Flows full to flood that fills
From the arch of air it thrills
Those rust-red iron hills
With morning up.

Dawn, as a panther springs,
With fierce and fire-fledged wings
Leaps on the land that rings
From her bright feet
Through all its lava-black
Cones that cast answer back
And cliffs of footless track
Where thunders meet.

The light speaks wide and loud
From deeps blown clean of cloud
As though day's heart were proud
And heaven's were glad;
The towers brown-striped and grey
Take fire from heaven of day
As though the prayers they pray
Their answers had.

Higher in these high first hours
Wax all the keen church towers,
And higher all hearts of ours
Than the old hills' crown,
Higher than the pillared height
Of that strange cliff-side bright
With basalt towers whose might
Strong time bows down.

And the old fierce ruin there
Of the old wild princes' lair
Whose blood in mine hath share
Gapes gaunt and great
Toward heaven that long ago
Watched all the wan land's woe
Whereon the wind would blow
Of their bleak hate.

Dead are those deeds; but yet
Their memory seems to fret
Lands that might else forget
That old world's brand;
Dead all their sins and days;
Yet in this red clime's rays
Some fiery memory stays

That sears their land.

IV. AUTUMN IN CORNWALL

The year lies fallen and faded
On cliffs by clouds invaded,
With tongues of storms upbraided,
With wrath of waves bedinned;
And inland, wild with warning,
As in deaf ears or scorning,
The clarion even and morning
Rings of the south-west wind.

The wild bents wane and wither
In blasts whose breath bows hither
Their grey-grown heads and thither,
Unblest of rain or sun;
The pale fierce heavens are crowded
With shapes like dreams beclouded,
As though the old year enshrouded
Lay, long ere life were done.

Full-charged with oldworld wonders,
From dusk Tintagel thunders
A note that smites and sunders
The hard frore fields of air;
A trumpet stormier-sounded
Than once from lists rebounded
When strong men sense-confounded
Fell thick in tourney there.

From scarce a duskier dwelling
Such notes of wail rose welling
Through the outer darkness, telling
In the awful singer's ears
What souls the darkness covers,
What love-lost souls of lovers,
Whose cry still hangs and hovers
In each man's born that hears.

For there by Hector's brother
And yet some thousand other
He that had grief to mother
Passed pale from Dante's sight;
With one fast linked as fearless,
Perchance, there only tearless;
Iseult and Tristram, peerless

And perfect queen and knight.

A shrill-winged sound comes flying
North, as of wild souls crying
The cry of things undying,
That know what life must be;
Or as the old year's heart, stricken
Too sore for hope to quicken
By thoughts like thorns that thicken,
Broke, breaking with the sea.

THE WHITE CZAR

[In an English magazine of 1877 there appeared a version of some insolent lines addressed by "A Russian Poet to the Empress of India." To these the first of the two following sonnets was designed to serve by way of counterblast. The writer will scarcely be suspected of royalism or imperialism; but it seemed to him that an insult levelled by Muscovite lips at the ruler of England might perhaps be less unfitly than unofficially resented by an Englishman who was also a republican.]

I

Gehazi by the hue that chills thy cheek
And Pilate by the hue that sears thine hand
Whence all earth's waters cannot wash the brand
That signs thy soul a manslayer's though thou speak
All Christ, with lips most murderous and most meek—
Thou set thy foot where England's used to stand!
Thou reach thy rod forth over Indian land!
Slave of the slaves that call thee lord, and weak
As their foul tongues who praise thee! son of them
Whose presence put the snows and stars to shame
In centuries dead and damned that reek below
Curse-consecrated, crowned with crime and flame,
To them that bare thee like them shalt thou go
Forth of man's life—a leper white as snow.

II

Call for clear water, wash thine hands, be clean,
Cry, What is truth? O Pilate; thou shalt know
Haply too soon, and gnash thy teeth for woe
Ere the outer darkness take thee round unseen
That hides the red ghosts of thy race obscene
Bound nine times round with hell's most dolorous flow,
And in its pools thy crownless head lie low

By his of Spain who dared an English queen
With half a world to hearten him for fight,
Till the wind gave his warriors and their might
To shipwreck and the corpse-encumbered sea.
But thou, take heed, ere yet thy lips wax white,
Lest as it was with Philip so it be,
O white of name and red of hand, with thee.

RIZPAH

How many sons, how many generations,
For how long years hast thou bewept, and known
Nor end of torment nor surcease of moan,
Rachel or Rizpah, wofullest of nations,
Crowned with the crowning sign of desolations,
And couldst not even scare off with hand or groan
Those carrion birds devouring bone by bone
The children of thy thousand tribulations?
Thou wast our warrior once; thy sons long dead
Against a foe less foul than this made head,
Poland, in years that sound and shine afar;
Ere the east beheld in thy bright sword-blade's stead
The rotten corpse-light of the Russian star
That lights towards hell his bondslaves and their Czar.

TO LOUIS KOSSUTH

1877

Light of our fathers' eyes, and in our own
Star of the unsetting sunset! for thy name,
That on the front of noon was as a flame
In the great year nigh thirty years agone
When all the heavens of Europe shook and shone
With stormy wind and lightning, keeps its fame
And bears its witness all day through the same;
Not for past days and great deeds past alone,
Kossuth, we praise thee as our Landor praised,
But that now too we know thy voice upraised,
Thy voice, the trumpet of the truth of God,
Thine hand, the thunder-bearer's, raised to smite
As with heaven's lightning for a sword and rod
Men's heads abased before the Muscovite.

THE COMPLAINT OF THE FAIR ARMOURESS

I

Meseemeth I heard cry and groan
That sweet who was the armourer's maid;
For her young years she made sore moan,
And right upon this wise she said;
"Ah fierce old age with foul bald head,
To spoil fair things thou art over fain;
Who holdeth me? who? would God I were dead!
Would God I were well dead and slain!

II

"Lo, thou hast broken the sweet yoke
That my high beauty held above
All priests and clerks and merchant-folk;
There was not one but for my love
Would give me gold and gold enough,
Though sorrow his very heart had riven,
To win from me such wage thereof
As now no thief would take if given.

III

"I was right chary of the same,
God wot it was my great folly,
For love of one sly knave of them,
Good store of that same sweet had he;
For all my subtle wiles, perdie,
God wot I loved him well enow;
Right evilly he handled me,
But he loved well my gold, I trow.

IV

"Though I gat bruises green and black,
I loved him never the less a jot;
Though he bound burdens on my back,
If he said 'Kiss me and heed it not'

Right little pain I felt, God wot,
When that foul thief's mouth, found so sweet,
Kissed me—Much good thereof I got!
I keep the sin and the shame of it.

V

"And he died thirty year agone.
I am old now, no sweet thing to see;
By God, though, when I think thereon,
And of that good glad time, woe's me,
And stare upon my changed body
Stark naked, that has been so sweet,
Lean, wizen, like a small dry tree,
I am nigh mad with the pain of it.

VI

"Where is my faultless forehead's white,
The lifted eyebrows, soft gold hair,
Eyes wide apart and keen of sight,
With subtle skill in the amorous air;
The straight nose, great nor small, but fair,
The small carved ears of shapeliest growth,
Chin dimpling, colour good to wear,
And sweet red splendid kissing mouth?

VII

"The shapely slender shoulders small,
Long arms, hands wrought in glorious wise,
Round little breasts, the hips withal
High, full of flesh, not scant of size,
Fit for all amorous masteries;
The large loin, and the flower that was
Planted above my strong round thighs
In a small garden of soft grass.

VIII

"A writhled forehead, hair gone grey,
Fallen eyebrows, eyes gone blind and red,
Their laughs and looks all fled away,
Yea, all that smote men's hearts are fled;

The bowed nose, fallen from goodlihead;
Foul flapping ears like water-flags;
Peaked chin, and cheeks all waste and dead,
And lips that are two skinny rags:

IX

"Thus endeth all the beauty of us.
The arms made short, the hands made lean,
The shoulders bowed and ruinous,
The breasts, alack! all fallen in;
The flanks too, like the breasts, grown thin;
As for the sweet place, out on it!
For the lank thighs, no thighs but skin,
They are specked with spots like sausage-meat.

X

"So we make moan for the old sweet days,
Poor old light women, two or three
Squatting above the straw-fire's blaze,
The bosom crushed against the knee,
Like faggots on a heap we be,
Round fires soon lit, soon quenched and done;
And we were once so sweet, even we!
Thus fareth many and many an one."

A DOUBLE BALLAD OF GOOD COUNSEL

Now take your fill of love and glee,
And after balls and banquets hie;
In the end ye'll get no good for fee,
But just heads broken by and by;
Light loves make beasts of men that sigh;
They changed the faith of Solomon,
And left not Samson lights to spy;
Good luck has he that deals with none!

Sweet Orpheus, lord of minstrelsy,
For this with flute and pipe came nigh
The danger of the dog's heads three
That ravening at hell's door doth lie;
Fain was Narcissus, fair and shy,
For love's love lightly lost and won,

In a deep well to drown and die;
Good luck has he that deals with none!

Sardana, flower of chivalry,
Who conquered Crete with horn and cry,
For this was fain a maid to be
And learn with girls the thread to ply;
King David, wise in prophecy,
Forgot the fear of God for one
Seen washing either shapely thigh;
Good luck has he that deals with none!

For this did Amnon, craftily
Feigning to eat of cakes of rye,
Deflower his sister fair to see,
Which was foul incest; and hereby
Was Herod moved, it is no lie,
To lop the head of Baptist John
For dance and jig and psaltery;
Good luck has he that deals with none!

Next of myself I tell, poor me,
How thrashed like clothes at wash was I
Stark naked, I must needs agree;
Who made me eat so sour a pie
But Katherine of Vaucelles? thereby,
Noé took third part of that fun;
Such wedding-gloves are ill to buy;
Good luck has he that deals with none!

But for that young man fair and free
To pass those young maids lightly by,
Nay, would you burn him quick, not he;
Like broom-horsed witches though he fry,
They are sweet as civet in his eye;
But trust them, and you're fooled anon;
For white or brown, and low or high,
Good luck has he that deals with none!

FRAGMENT ON DEATH

And Paris be it or Helen dying,
Who dies soever, dies with pain.
He that lacks breath and wind for sighing,
His gall bursts on his heart; and then
He sweats, God knows what sweat!—again,

No man may ease him of his grief;
Child, brother, sister, none were fain
To bail him thence for his relief.

Death makes him shudder, swoon, wax pale,
Nose bend, veins stretch, and breath surrender,
Neck swell, flesh soften, joints that fail
Crack their strained nerves and arteries slender.
O woman's body found so tender,
Smooth, sweet, so precious in men's eyes,
Must thou too bear such count to render?
Yes; or pass quick into the skies.

[In the original here follows Villon's masterpiece, the matchless Ballad of the Ladies of Old Time, so incomparably rendered in the marvelous version of D. G. Rossetti; followed in its turn by the succeeding poem, as inferior to its companion as is my attempt at translation of it to his triumph in that higher and harder field.—A. C. S.]

BALLAD OF THE LORDS OF OLD TIME

(AFTER THE FORMER ARGUMENT)

What more? Where is the third Calixt,
Last of that name now dead and gone,
Who held four years the Papalist?
Alphonso king of Aragon,
The gracious lord, duke of Bourbon,
And Arthur, duke of old Britaine?
And Charles the Seventh, that worthy one?
Even with the good knight Charlemain.

The Scot too, king of mount and mist,
With half his face vermilion,
Men tell us, like an amethyst
From brow to chin that blazed and shone;
The Cypriote king of old renown,
Alas! and that good king of Spain,
Whose name I cannot think upon?
Even with the good knight Charlemain.

No more to say of them I list;
'Tis all but vain, all dead and done:
For death may no man born resist,
Nor make appeal when death comes on.
I make yet one more question;

Where's Lancelot, king of far Bohain?
Where's he whose grandson called him son?
Even with the good knight Charlemain.

Where is Guesclin, the good Breton?
The lord of the eastern mountain-chain,
And the good late duke of Alençon?
Even with the good knight Charlemain.

BALLAD OF THE WOMEN OF PARIS

Albeit the Venice girls get praise
For their sweet speech and tender air,
And though the old women have wise ways
Of chaffering for amorous ware,
Yet at my peril dare I swear,
Search Rome, where God's grace mainly tarries,
Florence and Savoy, everywhere,
There's no good girl's lip out of Paris.

The Naples women, as folk prattle,
Are sweetly spoken and subtle enough:
German girls are good at tattle,
And Prussians make their boast thereof;
Take Egypt for the next remove,
Or that waste land the Tartar harries,
Spain or Greece, for the matter of love,
There's no good girl's lip out of Paris.

Breton and Swiss know nought of the matter,
Gascony girls or girls of Toulouse;
Two fishwives here with a half-hour's chatter
Would shut them up by threes and twos;
Calais, Lorraine, and all their crews,
(Names enow the mad song marries)
England and Picardy, search them and choose,
There's no good girl's lip out of Paris.

Prince, give praise to our French ladies
For the sweet sound their speaking carries;
'Twixt Rome and Cadiz many a maid is,
But no good girl's lip out of Paris.

BALLAD WRITTEN FOR A BRIDEGROOM

WHICH VILLON GAVE TO A GENTLEMAN NEWLY MARRIED TO SEND TO HIS WIFE WHOM HE HAD WON
WITH THE SWORD

At daybreak, when the falcon claps his wings,
No whit for grief, but noble heart and high,
With loud glad noise he stirs himself and springs,
And takes his meat and toward his lure draws nigh;
Such good I wish you! Yea, and heartily
I am fired with hope of true love's meed to get;
Know that Love writes it in his book; for why,
This is the end for which we twain are met.

Mine own heart's lady with no gainsayings
You shall be always wholly till I die;
And in my right against all bitter things
Sweet laurel with fresh rose its force shall try;
Seeing reason wills not that I cast love by
(Nor here with reason shall I chide or fret)
Nor cease to serve, but serve more constantly;
This is the end for which we twain are met.

And, which is more, when grief about me clings
Through Fortune's fit or fume of jealousy,
Your sweet kind eye beats down her threatenings
As wind doth smoke; such power sits in your eye.
Thus in your field my seed of harvestry
Thrives, for the fruit is like me that I set;
God bids me tend it with good husbandry;
This is the end for which we twain are met.

Princess, give ear to this my summary;
That heart of mine your heart's love should forget
Shall never be: like trust in you put I:
This is the end for which we twain are met.

BALLAD AGAINST THE ENEMIES OF FRANCE

May he fall in with beasts that scatter fire,
Like Jason, when he sought the fleece of gold,
Or change from man to beast three years entire,
As King Nebuchadnezzar did of old;
Or else have times as shameful and as bad
As Trojan folk for ravished Helen had;
Or gulfed with Proserpine and Tantalus
Let hell's deep fen devour him dolorous,

With worse to bear than Job's worst sufferance,
Bound in his prison-maze with Dædalus,
Who could wish evil to the state of France!

May he four months, like bitterns in the mire,
Howl with head downmost in the lake-springs cold,
Or to bear harness like strong bulls for hire
To the Great Turk for money down be sold;
Or thirty years like Magdalen live sad,
With neither wool nor web of linen clad;
Drown like Narciss', or swing down pendulous
Like Absalom with locks luxurious,
Or liker Judas fallen to reprobance;
Or find such death as Simon sorcerous,
Who could wish evil to the state of France!

May the old times come of fierce Octavian's ire,
And in his belly molten coin be told;
May he like Victor in the mill expire,
Crushed between moving millstones on him rolled,
Or in deep sea drenched breathless, more adrad
Than in the whale's bulk Jonas, when God bade:
From Phoebus' light, from Juno's treasure-house
Driven, and from joys of Venus amorous,
And cursed of God most high to the utterance,
As was the Syrian king Antiochus,
Who could wish evil to the state of France!

Prince, may the bright-winged brood of Æolus
To sea-king Glaucus' wild wood cavernous
Bear him bereft of peace and hope's least glance,
For worthless is he to get good of us,
Who could wish evil to the state of France.

THE DISPUTE OF THE HEART AND BODY OF FRANÇOIS VILLON

Who is this I hear?—Lo, this is I, thine heart,
That holds on merely now by a slender string.
Strength fails me, shape and sense are rent apart,
The blood in me is turned to a bitter thing,
Seeing thee skulk here like a dog shivering.—
Yea, and for what?—For that thy sense found sweet.—
What irks it thee?—I feel the sting of it.—
Leave me at peace.—Why?—Nay now, leave me at peace;
I will repent when I grow ripe in wit.—
I say no more.—I care not though thou cease.—

What art thou, trow?—A man worth praise, perfay.—
This is thy thirtieth year of wayfaring.—
'Tis a mule's age.—Art thou a boy still?—Nay.—
Is it hot lust that spurs thee with its sting,
Grasping thy throat? Know'st thou not anything?—
Yea, black and white, when milk is specked with flies,
I can make out.—No more?—Nay, in no wise.
Shall I begin again the count of these?—
Thou art undone.—I will make shift to rise.—
I say no more.—I care not though thou cease.—

I have the sorrow of it, and thou the smart.
Wert thou a poor mad fool or weak of wit,
Then might'st thou plead this pretext with thine heart;
But if thou know not good from evil a whit,
Either thy head is hard as stone to hit,
Or shame, not honour, gives thee most content.
What canst thou answer to this argument?—
When I am dead I shall be well at ease.—
God! what good hope!—Thou art over eloquent.—
I say no more.—I care not though thou cease.—

Whence is this ill?—From sorrow and not from sin.
When Saturn packed my wallet up for me
I well believe he put these ills therein.—
Fool, wilt thou make thy servant lord of thee?
Hear now the wise king's counsel; thus saith he:
All power upon the stars a wise man hath;
There is no planet that shall do him scathe.—
Nay, as they made me I grow and I decrease.—
What say'st thou?—Truly this is all my faith.—
I say no more.—I care not though thou cease.—

Wouldst thou live still?—God help me that I may!—
Then thou must—What? turn penitent and pray?—
Read always—What?—Grave words and good to say;
Leave off the ways of fools, lest they displease.—
Good; I will do it.—Wilt thou remember?—Yea.—
Abide not till there come an evil day.
I say no more.—I care not though thou cease.

EPISTLE IN FORM OF A BALLAD TO HIS FRIENDS

Have pity, pity, friends, have pity on me,
Thus much at least, may it please you, of your grace!

I lie not under hazel or hawthorn-tree
Down in this dungeon ditch, mine exile's place
By leave of God and fortune's foul disgrace.
Girls, lovers, glad young folk and newly wed,
Jumpers and jugglers, tumbling heel o'er head,
Swift as a dart, and sharp as needle-ware,
Throats clear as bells that ring the kine to shed,
Your poor old friend, what, will you leave him there?

Singers that sing at pleasure, lawlessly,
Light, laughing, gay of word and deed, that race
And run like folk light-witted as ye be
And have in hand nor current coin nor base,
Ye wait too long, for now he's dying apace.
Rhymers of lays and roundels sung and read,
Ye'll brew him broth too late when he lies dead.
Nor wind nor lightning, sunbeam nor fresh air,
May pierce the thick wall's bound where lies his bed;
Your poor old friend, what, will you leave him there?

O noble folk from tithes and taxes free,
Come and behold him in this piteous case,
Ye that nor king nor emperor holds in fee,
But only God in heaven; behold his face
Who needs must fast, Sundays and holidays,
Which makes his teeth like rakes; and when he hath fed
With never a cake for banquet but dry bread,
Must drench his bowels with much cold watery fare,
With board nor stool, but low on earth instead;
Your poor old friend, what, will you leave him there?

Princes afore-named, old and young foresaid,
Get me the king's seal and my pardon sped,
And hoist me in some basket up with care:
So swine will help each other ill bested,
For where one squeaks they run in heaps ahead.
Your poor old friend, what, will you leave him there?

THE EPITAPH IN FORM OF A BALLAD

WHICH VILLON MADE FOR HIMSELF AND HIS COMRADES, EXPECTING TO BE HANGED ALONG WITH
THEM

Men, brother men, that after us yet live,
Let not your hearts too hard against us be;
For if some pity of us poor men ye give,

The sooner God shall take of you pity.
Here are we five or six strung up, you see,
And here the flesh that all too well we fed
Bit by bit eaten and rotten, rent and shred,
And we the bones grow dust and ash withal;
Let no man laugh at us discomforted,
But pray to God that he forgive us all.

If we call on you, brothers, to forgive,
Ye should not hold our prayer in scorn, though we
Were slain by law; ye know that all alive
Have not wit alway to walk righteously;
Make therefore intercession heartily
With him that of a virgin's womb was bred,
That his grace be not as a dry well-head
For us, nor let hell's thunder on us fall;
We are dead, let no man harry or vex us dead,
But pray to God that he forgive us all.

The rain has washed and laundered us all five,
And the sun dried and blackened; yea, perdie,
Ravens and pies with beaks that rend and rive
Have dug our eyes out, and plucked off for fee
Our beards and eyebrows; never are we free,
Not once, to rest; but here and there still sped,
Drive at its wild will by the wind's change led,
More pecked of birds than fruits on garden-wall;
Men, for God's love, let no gibe here be said,
But pray to God that he forgive us all.

Prince Jesus, that of all art lord and head,
Keep us, that hell be not our bitter bed;
We have nought to do in such a master's hall.
Be not ye therefore of our fellowhead,
But pray to God that he forgive us all.

FROM VICTOR HUGO

Take heed of this small child of earth;
He is great: he hath in him God most high.
Children before their fleshly birth
Are lights alive in the blue sky.

In our light bitter world of wrong
They come; God gives us them awhile.
His speech is in their stammering tongue,

And his forgiveness in their smile.

Their sweet light rests upon our eyes.
Alas! their right to joy is plain.
If they are hungry, Paradise
Weeps, and, if cold, Heaven thrills with pain.

The want that saps their sinless flower
Speaks judgment on sin's ministers.
Man holds an angel in his power.
Ah! deep in Heaven what thunder stirs,

When God seeks out these tender things
Whom in the shadow where we sleep
He sends us clothed about with wings,
And finds them ragged babes that weep!

NOCTURNE

La nuit écoute et se penche sur l'onde
Pour y cueillir rien qu'un souffle d'amour;
Pas de lueur, pas de musique au monde,
Pas de sommeil pour moi ni de séjour.
O mère, ô Nuit, de ta source profonde
Verse-nous, verse enfin l'oubli du jour.

Verse l'oubli de l'angoisse et du jour;
Chante; ton chant assoupit l'âme et l'onde:
Fais de ton sein pour mon âme un séjour,
Elle est bien lasse, ô mère, de ce monde,
Où le baiser ne veut pas dire amour,
Où l'âme aimée est moins que toi profonde.

Car toute chose aimée est moins profonde,
O Nuit, que toi, fille et mère du jour;
Toi dont l'attente est le répit du monde,
Toi dont le souffle est plein de mots d'amour,
Toi dont l'haleine enfle et réprime l'onde,
Toi dont l'ombre a tout le ciel pour séjour.

La misère humble et lasse, sans séjour,
S'abrite et dort sous ton aile profonde;
Tu fais à tous l'aumône de l'amour:
Toutes les soifs viennent boire à ton onde,
Tout ce qui pleure et se dérobe au jour,
Toutes les faims et tous les maux du monde.

Moi seul je veille et ne vois dans ce monde
Que ma douleur qui n'ait point de séjour
Où s'abriter sur ta rive profonde
Et s'endormir sous tes yeux loin du jour;
Je vais toujours cherchant au bord de l'onde
Le sang du beau pied blessé de l'amour.

La mer est sombre où tu naquis, amour,
Pleine des pleurs et des sanglots du monde;
On ne voit plus le gouffre où naît le jour
Luire et frémir sous ta lueur profonde;
Mais dans les coeurs d'homme où tu fais séjour
La douleur monte et baisse comme une onde.

ENVOI

Fille de l'onde et mère de l'amour,
Du haut séjour plein de ta paix profonde
Sur ce bas monde épands un peu de jour.

THÉOPHILE GAUTIER

Pour mettre une couronne au front d'une chanson,
Il semblait qu'en passant son pied semât des roses,
Et que sa main cueillît comme des fleurs écloses
Les étoiles au fond du ciel en floraison.

Sa parole de marbre et d'or avait le son
Des clairons de l'été chassant les jours moroses;
Comme en Thrace Apollon banni des grands cieux roses,
Il regardait du coeur l'Olympe, sa maison.

Le soleil fut pour lui le soleil du vieux monde,
Et son oeil recherchait dans les flots embrasés
Le sillon immortel d'où s'élança sur l'onde
Vénus, que la mer molle enivrait de baisers:
Enfin, dieu ressaisi de sa splendeur première,
Il trône, et son sépulcre est bâti de lumière.

ODE (LE TOMBEAU DE THÉOPHILE GAUTIER)

Quelle fleur, ô Mort, quel joyau, quel chant,

Quel vent, quel rayon de soleil couchant,
Sur ton front penché, sur ta main avide,
Sur l'âpre pâleur de ta lèvre aride,
Vibre encore et luit?
Ton sein est sans lait, ton oreille est vide,
Ton oeil plein de nuit.

Ta bouche est sans souffle et ton front sans ride;
Mais l'éclair voilé d'une flamme humide,
Flamme éclose au coeur d'un ciel pluvieux,
Rallume ta lèvre et remplit tes yeux
De lueurs d'opale;
Ta bouche est vermeille et ton front joyeux,
O toi qui fus pâle.

Comme aux jours divins la mère des dieux,
Reine au sein fécond, au corps radieux,
Tu surgis au bord de la tombe amère;
Tu nous apparais, ô Mort, vierge et mère,
Effroi des humains,
Le divin laurier sur la tête altière
Et la lyre aux mains.

Nous reconnaissons, courbés vers la terre,
Que c'est la splendeur de ta face austère
Qui dore la nuit de nos longs malheurs;
Que la vie ailée aux mille couleurs,
Dont tu n'es que l'âme,
Refait par tes mains les prés et les fleurs,
La rose et la femme.

Lune constante! astre ami des douleurs
Qui luis à travers la brume des pleurs!
Quelle flamme au fond de ta clarté molle
Éclate et rougit, nouvelle auréole,
Ton doux front voilé?
Quelle étoile, ouvrant ses ailes, s'envole
Du ciel étoilé?

Pleurant ce rayon de jour qu'on lui vole,
L'homme exècre en vain la Mort triste et folle;
Mais l'astre qui fut à nos yeux si beau,
Là-haut, loin d'ici, dans un ciel nouveau
Plein d'autres étoiles,
Se lève, et pour lui la nuit du tombeau
Entr'ouvre ses voiles.

L'âme est dans le corps comme un jeune oiseau

Dont l'aile s'agite au bord du berceau;
La mort, déliant cette aile inquiète,
Quand nous écoutons la bouche muette
Qui nous dit adieu,
Fait de l'homme infime et sombre un poëte,
Du poëte un dieu.

IN OBITUM THEOPHILI POETÆ

O lux Pieridum et laurigeri deliciæ dei,
Vox leni Zephyro lenior, ut veris amans novi
Tollit floridulis implicitum primitiis caput,
Ten' ergo abripuit non rediturum, ut redeunt novo
Flores vere novi, te quoque mors irrevocabilem?
Cur vatem neque te Musa parens, te neque Gratiæ,
Nec servare sibi te potuit fidum animi Venus?
Quæ nunc ipsa magis vel puero te Cinyreïo,
Te desiderium et flebilibus lumen amoribus,
Amissum queritur, sanguineis fusa comam genis.
Tantis tu lacrymis digne, comes dulcis Apollini,
Carum nomen eris dîs superis atque sodalibus
Nobis, quîs eadem quæ tibi vivo patuit via
Non æquis patet, at te sequimur passibus haud tuis,
At mæsto cinerem carmine non illacrymabilem
Tristesque exuvias floribus ac fletibus integris
Unà contegimus, nec citharâ nec sine tibiâ,
Votoque unanimæ vocis Ave dicimus et Vale.

AD CATULLUM

Catulle frater, ut velim comes tibi
Remota per vireta, per cavum nemus
Sacrumque Ditis haud inhospiti specus,
Pedem referre, trans aquam Stygis ducem
Secutus unum et unicum, Catulle, te,
Ut ora vatis optimi reviserem,
Tui meique vatis ora, quem scio
Venustiorem adîsse vel tuo lacum,
Benigniora semper arva vel tuis,
Ubi serenus accipit suos deus,
Tegitque myrtus implicata laureâ,
Manuque mulcet halituque consecrat
Fovetque blanda mors amabili sinu,
Et ore fama fervido colit viros

Alitque qualis unus ille par tibi
Britannus unicusque in orbe præstitit
Amicus ille noster, ille ceteris
Poeta major, omnibusque floribus
Priore Landor inclytum rosâ caput
Revinxit extulitque, quam tuâ manu
Recepit ac refovit integram suâ.

1878

Some nine years gone, as we dwelt together
In the sweet hushed heat of the south French weather
Ere autumn fell on the vine-tressed hills
Or the season had shed one rose-red feather,

Friend, whose fame is a flame that fills
All eyes it lightens and hearts it thrills
With joy to be born of the blood which bred
From a land that the grey sea girds and chills

The heart and spirit and hand and head
Whose might is as light on a dark day shed,
On a day now dark as a land's decline
Where all the peers of your praise are dead,

In a land and season of corn and vine
I pledged you a health from a beaker of mine
But halfway filled to the lip's edge yet
With hope for honey and song for wine.

Nine years have risen and eight years set
Since there by the wellspring our hands on it met:
And the pledge of my songs that were then to be,
I could wonder not, friend, though a friend should forget.

For life's helm rocks to the windward and lee,
And time is as wind, and as waves are we;
And song is as foam that the sea-winds fret,
Though the thought at its heart should be deep as the sea.

Algernon Charles Swinburne was born at 7 Chester Street, Grosvenor Place, in London, on April 5th, 1837. He was the eldest of six children born to Captain Charles Henry Swinburne and Lady Jane Henrietta, daughter of the 3rd Earl of Ashburnham, a wealthy Northumbrian family.

Swinburne spent his early years at East Dene in Bonchurch, on the Isle of Wight. As a child, Swinburne was nervous and frail, but also imbued with a nervous energy and fearlessness almost to the point of recklessness.

He was schooled at Eton College from 1849 to 1853. It was here that he first began to write poetry. He excelled at languages and whilst still at Eton won first prizes in both French and Italian.

From Eton he moved to Oxford where he attended at Balliol College from 1856. Here he met friends to whom he became closely attached, among them Dante Gabriel Rossetti, William Morris and Edward Burne-Jones, who in 1857, were painting their Arthurian murals on the walls of the Oxford Union. At Oxford Swinburne was mentored by Benjamin Jowett, the master of Balliol College, who recognised his poetic talent and, intervening on his behalf, tried to keep him from being expelled when he celebrated the Italian patriot Orsini, and his failed attempt on the life of Napoleon III in 1858. Swinburne had to leave the Universcity for a few months due to this but returned in May, 1860 but never received a degree.

Summers were usually spent at Capheaton Hall in Northumberland, the house of his grandfather, Sir John Swinburne, 6th Baronet, who had a famous library and was himself President of the Literary and Philosophical Society in Newcastle upon Tyne.

Swinburne proudly considered himself a native of Northumberland and this is reflected in poems such as the intensely patriotic 'Northumberland' and 'Grace Darling'. He enjoyed riding across the moors and was, it was said, a daring horseman, as he moved 'through honeyed leagues of the northland border', as he remembered the Scottish border in his Recollections.

In the period from 1857 to 1860, Swinburne was one of a number of Pre-Raphaelite's who visited and became part of Lady Pauline Trevelyan's intellectual circle at Wallington Hall, a few miles west of Morpeth in Northumberland.

After leaving college, he moved to London and began his career in earnest as well as becoming a constant visitor to the Rossetti's house. To Rossetti Swinburne was his 'little Northumbrian friend', an affectionate reference to Swinburne's small stature—a mere five foot four. Whatever Swinburne lacked in height he made up for in poetic talent. However, with the burden of such great talent came the unveiling of a dark side that was to cause him pain and would, at times, threaten his very existence with all manner of self-inflicted pains through drink, drugs and sado-machoism.

In 1860 Swinburne published two verse dramas; The Queen Mother and Rosamond but it would not be until 1865 that Swinburne would achieve literary success with Atalanta in Calydon.

In 1861, Swinburne visited Menton on the French Riviera to recover from the effects of yet another period of excess use of alcohol, staying at the Villa Laurenti. From Menton, Swinburne then travelled on to Italy, where he journeyed widely.

After Elizabeth Rossetti's death from suicide in 1862, he and Rossetti moved to Tudor House at 16 Cheyne Walk in Chelsea. The stories that survive from his year with Rossetti are typical Swinburne. In one, Rossetti once had to tell him to keep down the noise — he and a boyfriend had been sliding naked down the bannisters and disturbing Rossetti's painting. He took a sardonic delight in what the critic and biographer, Cecil Lang, calls "Algernonic exaggeration": When people began to talk scathingly about his homosexuality and other sexual proclivities, he circulated a story that he had engaged in pederasty and bestiality with a monkey — and then eaten it. How many of the stories were true and how many invented is unclear. Oscar Wilde called him "a braggart in matters of vice, who had done everything he could to convince his fellow citizens of his homosexuality and bestiality without being in the slightest degree a homosexual or a bestialiser."

In December 1862, Swinburne accompanied Scott and his guests on a trip to Tynemouth. Scott writes in his memoirs that, as they walked by the sea, Swinburne declaimed the as yet unpublished 'Hymn to Proserpine' and 'Laus Veneris' in his lilting intonation, while the waves 'were running the whole length of the long level sands towards Cullercoats and sounding like far-off acclamations'.

Swinburne possessed a curious combination of frail health and strength. He was small and slightly built, but an excellent swimmer and the first to climb Culver Cliff on the Isle of Wight. He had an extremely excitable disposition: people who met him described him as a "demoniac boy" who would go skipping about the room declaiming poetry at the top of his voice. In this as in many things, moderation was not the standard for him. Excess was. Once or twice he had fits, thought to be epileptic, in public; but he made this condition much worse by drinking past excess to unconsciousness. More than once he was delivered to the door in the small of the night, dead drunk. Throughout the 1860s and '70s he rode an alcoholic cycle of dissolution, collapse, drying out at home in the country, then returning to London where he would begin the cycle all over again.

His mania for masochism, particularly flagellation, most probably started in early childhood at Eton and was encouraged by his later friendships with Richard Monckton Milnes (one of Tennyson's fellow Apostles), who introduced him to the works of the Marquis de Sade, and Richard Burton, the Victorian explorer and adventurer. Swinburne was an alcoholic and algolagniac (a desire for sexual gratification through inflicting pain on oneself or others; sadomasochism). He found life difficult, unfulfilling but still his poetic talents pushed to the fore.

Although Swinburne continued to publish some works in periodicals in 1865 he was granted recognition by both public and critics with Atalanta in Calydon written in the style of a classical Greek tragedy.

There followed "Laus Veneris" and Poems and Ballads (1866), with their sexually charged passages, absolutely decadent for polite Victorian society, which were attacked all the more violently as a result. The poems written in homage of Sappho of Lesbos such as "Anactoria" and "Sapphics" were especially savaged. The volume also contained poems such as "The Leper," "Laus Veneris," and "St Dorothy" which evoke both Swinburne's and a general Victorian fascination with the Middle Ages, and are explicitly mediaeval in style, tone and construction. With its publication came instant notoriety. He was now identified with indecent and decadent themes and the precept of art for art's sake.

Swinburne's meeting in 1867 with his long-time hero Mazzini, the Italian patriot living in England in exile, was the beginning of a poetical journey that now became more serious and more engaged with serious thought, initially leading to the political poems in the volume Songs Before Sunrise.

Also in 1867 he was introduced to Adah Isaacs Menken, the American actress, poet and circus rider, whose main fame seemed to be riding naked on a horse (in fact she wore tight nude coloured clothing) for her performance in the melodrama Mazeppa (itself based on a poem by Lord Byron). Although they had a short affair Adah's quote implies that Swinburne was not ready for a relationship that did not involve some self-sabotage; "I can't make him understand that biting's no use."

In 1879, with Swinburne nearly dead from alcoholism and dissolution, his legal advisor Theodore Watts-Dunton took him in, and was gradually successful in getting him to adapt to a healthier lifestyle. Swinburne lived the rest of his life at Watts-Dunton's house. He saw less and less of his old bohemian friends, who thought him a prisoner at The Pines, but his growing deafness also accounts for some of his decreased sociability. By now Swinburne was 42, and was moving from a young man of rebelliousness to a figure of social respectability. It was said of Watts-Dunton that he saved the man and killed the poet.

It is clear that Swinburne had an addictive personality, and clearly incapable of moderation in his pursuit of any chosen vices. This, of course, would both nourish and perhaps sabotage his poetic career. His poetry follows the somewhat clichéd pattern of early flourish and later decline; indeed some of the fresher pieces in the second and third series of Poems and Ballads (published in 1878 and 1889) were actually written during his days at Oxford. Nevertheless, his last collection, A Channel Passage, has some beautiful poems, including "The Lake of Gaube."

He is best remembered as the supreme technician in metre, with a versatility which exceeds even Tennyson's, but which lacks a corresponding emotional range. His obsessions are not widely enough shared; and if he cannot shock us by the strangeness of his desires nor the shrillness of his anti-theistical exclamations, often what remains is not enough to fully engage with the audience.

Swinburne is considered a poet of the decadent school, although he perhaps professed to more vice than he actually indulged in to advertise his deviance. Common gossip of the time reported that he also had a deep crush on the explorer Sir Richard Francis Burton, despite the fact that Swinburne himself abhorred travel. Fact and fiction are easily absorbed by the other so are difficult to untangle even now.

Many critics consider his mastery of vocabulary, rhyme and metre impressive, although he has also been criticised for his florid style and word choices that only fit the rhyme scheme rather than contributing to the meaning of the piece. A. E. Housman, although a critic, had great praise for his rhyming ability: to Swinburne the sonnet was child's play: the task of providing four rhymes was not hard enough, and he wrote long poems in which each stanza required eight or ten rhymes, and wrote them so that he never seemed to be saying anything for the rhyme's sake.

Throughout his career Swinburne published literary criticism of great worth. His deep knowledge of world literatures contributed to a critical style rich in quotation, allusion, and comparison. He is particularly noted for discerning studies of Elizabethan dramatists and of many English and French poets and novelists. As well he was a noted essayist and wrote two novels.

Swinburne was nominated for the Nobel Prize in Literature every year from 1903 to 1907 and then again in 1909.

H.P. Lovecraft, the master of the dark side and a decent poet himself, considered Swinburne "the only real poet in either England or America after the death of Mr. Edgar Allan Poe."

Swinburne was also responsible for devising a poetic form called the roundel, a variation of the French Rondeau form. In 1883 he published A Century of Roundels with several of the roundels dedicated to Dante's sister, the poet Christina Georgina Rossetti. Swinburne wrote to Edward Burne-Jones in 1883: "I have got a tiny new book of songs or songlets, in one form and all manner of metres ... just coming out, of which Miss Rossetti has accepted the dedication. I hope you and Georgie [his wife Georgiana] will find something to like among a hundred poems of nine lines each, twenty-four of which are about babies or small children".

Opinions of the Roundel poems move between those who find them captivating and brilliant, to others who find them merely clever and contrived. One of them, A Baby's Death, was set to music by the English composer Sir Edward Elgar as the song "Roundel: The little eyes that never knew Light".

After the first Poems and Ballads, Swinburne's later poetry was devoted more to philosophy and politics, including the unification of Italy, particularly in the volume Songs before Sunrise. He did not stop writing love poetry entirely, indeed it was only in 1882 that his great epic-length poem, Tristram of Lyonesse, was published, its contents lyrical rather than shocking. His versification, and especially his rhyming technique, remain of high quality to the end.

Algernon Charles Swinburne died of influenza, at the Pines in London on April 10th, 1909 at the age of 72. He was buried at St. Boniface Church, Bonchurch on the Isle of Wight.

Algernon Charles Swinburne – A Concise Bibliography

Verse Drama
The Queen Mother (1860)
Rosamond (1860)
Chastelard (1865)
Bothwell (1874)
Mary Stuart (1881)
Marino Faliero (1885)
Locrine (1887)
The Sisters (1892)
Rosamund, Queen of the Lombards (1899)

Poetry
Atalanta in Calydon (1865)*
Poems and Ballads (1866)
Songs Before Sunrise (1871)
Songs of Two Nations (1875)
Erechtheus (1876)*
Poems and Ballads, Second Series (1878)
Songs of the Springtides (1880)
Studies in Song (1880)
The Heptalogia, or the Seven against Sense. A Cap with Seven Bells (1880)
Tristram of Lyonesse (1882)
A Dark Month & Other Poems

A Century of Roundels (1883)
A Midsummer Holiday and Other Poems (1884)
Poems and Ballads, Third Series (1889)
Astrophel and Other Poems (1894)
The Tale of Balen (1896)
A Channel Passage and Other Poems (1904)

*Although formally tragedies, Atlanta in Calydon and Erechtheus are traditionally included with his poetry.

Criticism
William Blake: A Critical Essay (1868, new edition 1906)
Under the Microscope (1872)
George Chapman: A Critical Essay (1875)
Essays and Studies (1875)
A Note on Charlotte Brontë (1877)
A Study of Shakespeare (1880)
A Study of Victor Hugo (1886)
A Study of Ben Johnson (1889)
Studies in Prose and Poetry (1894)
The Age of Shakespeare (1908)
Shakespeare (1909)

Major Collections
The Poems of Algernon Charles Swinburne, 6 vols. 1904.
The Tragedies of Algernon Charles Swinburne, 5 vols. 1905.
The Complete Works of Algernon Charles Swinburne, 20 vols. Bonchurch Edition. 1925-7.
The Swinburne Letters, 6 vols. 1959-62.

www.ingramcontent.com/pod-product-compliance
Lightning Source LLC
Chambersburg PA
CBHW060129050426
42448CB00010B/2041